HOW TO HELP
YOUR TEENAGER
STOP SMOKING

HOW TO HELP
YOUR TEENAGER
STOP SMOKING

MICHAEL MANNION

WELCOME RAIN   **NEW YORK**

HOW TO HELP YOUR TEENAGER STOP SMOKING

Printed in the United States of America.

Direct any inquiries to

Welcome Rain Publishers LLC

532 Laguardia Place, Box 473

New York, NY 10012

Library of Congress Cataloging-in-Publication Data

Mannion, Michael T.

How to help your teenager stop smoking / Michael Mannion.

p.   cm.

Includes bibliographical references.

ISBN 1–56649–348–x (hardcover). — ISBN 1–56649–029–4 (pbk.)

1. Teenagers—Tobacco use—Prevention. 2. Tobacco habit—Prevention.

3. Smoking cessation programs.   I. Title.

HV5745.M325   1999

362.29'67'0835—dc21   99–39378

CIP

Manufactured in the United States of America by BLAZE I.P.I.

Text design by Victoria Kuskowski

First Edition: April 2000

1   3   5   7   9   10   8   6   4   2

CONTENTS

INTRODUCTION

A young mother is called at home one evening, after a hard day at work, and asked by the school guidance counselor to come to her office the next morning for a conference about her daughter, who has broken the school rules about smoking—again. But now the young teen has started cutting class to smoke. Not only does the single mother have to call her boss and hope he is not going to penalize her for being absent the next morning, but also, she is going to lose a badly needed half-day's pay as well. Her daughter had sworn on a stack of Bibles that she was no longer smoking.

.   .   .

A father finds that, once again, he seems to have less money in his wallet than he thought he had. Over the past few months, he has been coming up short a few days each week, a few dollars here, a few dollars there. But now it is adding up to $40 or $50 a month. He feels guilty because he suspects his son is taking the money to buy cigarettes. But his son has quit smoking. Or has he?

The above scenarios can be multiplied indefinitely. Every parent of a teen who smokes has had to deal with his or her teenager's lying, stealing small amounts of money, getting in trouble at school, and other problems related to smoking cigarettes. It can become extremely difficult for a parent to trust his or her teenager.

Your daughter or son finally seems serious about stopping smoking—but so what? Why should this time be any different? Instead of being happy, you are angry—perhaps really angry. There have been many attempts by your teenager to quit. There have been numerous lies told before, during, and after each failed attempt to quit. You have had it with your teen. You don't believe your teen anymore. Your anger is now much stronger than your love, concern, and support for your child. You may not show your anger overtly, but it is probably evident in your tone of voice and demeanor.

There is no way around these feelings of frustration and anger. You have to experience them. It does no good at all to suppress or repress them. It isn't who your child is that is driving you crazy, it is the behavior that is infuriating to you— namely smoking and not being honest about it. However, try to keep in mind that *feelings aren't facts*. Parents can't help but be angry at their teens' deceptions or disappointed at their failure to stop smoking. But it can help to put some facts alongside your feelings to get a balanced picture.

Fact: It takes 3 to 4 serious attempts, on average, for a smoker to quit. One study by the Hazelden Foundation showed that it took 10.8 attempts to quit smoking before success was achieved.

🚬 Your son or daughter has become addicted to a powerful drug.

- Nicotine is as powerful a drug as heroin or alcohol and many adults as well as teens fail repeatedly to get off these drugs.

- Teenagers have no idea whatsoever how easy it is to become addicted to cigarettes and no conception at all of how hard it is to quit smoking. It takes an average of 18.6 years for a smoker to quit successfully! Over this period, great physical harm—perhaps irreversible damage—will be done to your teenager's body.

- Very little is known about effective smoking cessation for teenagers. There are successful programs for adults, but teens pose a more difficult problem.

- Our society allows—even encourages and promotes—this potentially fatal addiction of your child to cigarettes, directly through clever, dishonest advertising and marketing schemes, and indirectly through the mass media.

Think about the enormous emotional influence the film *Titanic* has had on young teenage girls, for example. Hollywood films are once again saturated with images of stars—even young actors—smoking. Once again, smoking is glorified. In the film *Living Out Loud*, Hollywood star Holly Hunter smokes throughout the film. Look at the lines of teenagers outside of movie theaters waiting to get in and notice how many are lighting up.

Today, in 1999, adult smoking continues to decline. However, during the 1990s, there has been a startling dramatic rise in teenage smoking. Since 1991, there has been a 32 percent increase in smoking by high school students. In fact, 22 percent of high school seniors smoke everyday. Illness, disability, and premature death await these young people—perhaps your son or daughter—because of their addiction to a lethal but legal drug. One recent study of high school students in New Hampshire showed that almost 75 percent of the teens who smoked had never tried to quit. Over 80 percent of the teens told the researchers that they expected to be smoking a year later. Of these students, 31.9 percent smoked more than ten cigarettes a day and 23.6 percent smoked one to nine cigarettes. It is critical to help teenagers to stop smoking before cigarettes become an integral part of their self-image.

Your sons and daughters have been inundated with images of smoking from childhood on. Many teens, especially young teens, do not have the life experience to withstand the powerful forces that lure and pressure them to experiment with cigarettes. Although your teen's behavior may have caused you to become angry and to feel that you cannot trust your child anymore, put yourself in the youngster's shoes for a moment: She needs your help. Get past your anger, your lack of trust, and find the love and concern for your child that is in your heart. It may not be easy, but it is necessary.

What adult hasn't made a mistake, been dishonest, done something wrong, or been unable to live up to a resolution to give up a bad habit? If you can identify with what your teen is going through, you can get beyond the anger and lack of trust that frequently accompany a teenager's failed attempts to quit smoking.

It helps to talk openly about these feelings of anger, frustration, and lack of trust with your son or daughter. Not in a judgmental way, but in a forthright manner. Being honest with your child about your feelings is a sign of respect for your teenager, a sign that you expect the same in return.

If you can reach a state of mind where you look for progress, and not perfection, in your teenager who is struggling to quit smoking, the whole process will be easier on you and perhaps more successful for your daughter or son.

CHAPTER ONE
What Parents Need to Know

Your teenager needs you. As one fifteen-year-old girl succinctly put it during an interview conducted for this book, "We need our parents to share with us what they've learned." Parents of teens need all the help they can get when their teen becomes addicted to cigarettes. This book is a tool you can use to help your teenager quit smoking—when he or she wants to quit and is ready to accept help.

Quitting smoking may be the single most important thing anyone can do to improve his health. Helping a teenager quit smoking avoids years of unnecessary and life-threatening damage. Approximately 420,000 people die each year in the United States alone from cigarette-induced cancers. Tens of thousands more Americans die of other cigarette-caused diseases, such as emphysema, heart disease, stroke, and bronchitis. Disability and disease caused by smoking are the most unnecessary health problems we face today. And they are completely preventable—*if the smoker quits.* And the younger the smoker is when she quits, the better. Unfortunately, the problem of teenage smoking is not going to go away anytime soon. There is even evidence that things may get worse before they get better. Here are some startling facts to consider:

- About 91 percent of six-year-olds are as familiar with Joe Camel as they are with Mickey Mouse.
- Before Joe Camel, 3 percent of kids smoked; after Joe Camel, 25 percent of kids smoke.

- Children account for 90 percent of all new smokers.

- Smoking has increased by 50 percent among eighth-graders.

- Only 10 percent of smokers started when they were adults; 90 percent started as kids and the average age was twelve.

- Nearly one billion packs of cigarettes are sold illegally each year to boys and girls under eighteen.

- Nine out of ten times, kids can buy cigarettes from a vending machine; 50 percent of the time, kids can buy cigarettes in a store.

- Each year, one million U.S. teenagers start smoking—3,000 a day.

- Millions of today's teens will suffer severe health problems and die prematurely from cigarette-induced disease.

- From 1983–1993, the tobacco industry doubled its advertising budget, spending much of its $6 billion a year on activities and campaigns that appeal to young people.

Tobacco companies try to get their message out every way that they can. They have always done this. Everyone is a potential customer, no matter what age, race, religion, or sex. For example, during World War II, the tobacco companies convinced the military to give America's fighting men cigarettes as part of their rations. As a result, millions of veterans came home from the war addicted to cigarettes. Smoking rates in the United States doubled from 1940 to 1950. From 1945 to 1980, the lung cancer rate for American men increased fourfold. During that period, women were lured by clever tobacco company ads designed to make smoking look chic and sophisticated. Many women were soon addicted. From 1945 to 1980, the lung cancer rates for American women increased sevenfold. It was early in this era that cigarette advertisements even featured physicians who recommended smoking as a healthy habit for their patients.

Humphrey Bogart and John Wayne were both Hollywood tough guys and icons who smoked. Bogart died of lung cancer; Wayne lost one lung to cancer when he was in his early fifties. Teens today don't know the stars of yesteryear who promoted smoking in films, on TV, or in ads but who later died of cigarette-caused disease. Today, in 1998, it is estimated that 80 percent of male leads in movies smoke. Many of those stars who smoke in real life will be the cancer victims of tomorrow.

The tobacco industry also gets its wares into films by paying for a form of subliminal advertising called "product placement," a technique through which brand-name products appear in various scenes in major motion pictures. Studies have shown that people on TV and in the movies smoke far more than do people in the general population.

TV advertising was a powerful tool for the tobacco industry until the late 1960s. At that time, the FCC ruled that the TV networks had to accept antismoking ads. These commercials proved so effective in getting millions of people to quit smoking that the tobacco industry promised to no longer run TV commercials for its products, as long as no more antismoking ads were allowed on the air. Big Tobacco tried to portray its actions as being in the service of public health, but they had to get the powerful antismoking messages off TV as soon as possible. They were losing too much business.

One week after television commercials for cigarettes were off the air, the tobacco industry moved into magazine advertising in a big way. The week after the last TV ads were broadcast, *Life* magazine ran eleven pages of cigarette advertisements. Magazines and newspapers are still a major outlet for cigarette advertising. In fact, the line between advertisement and editorial may even be beginning to blur now. For example, the extremely popular 1998 *Sports Illustrated* "swimsuit" issue almost completely integrated the smoking advertising with the editorial copy and photographs of the supermodels, so that the cigarette advertising's models fit in smoothly. Both young men and women are influenced—consciously and unconsciously— by the powerful media images of the supermodels in the swimsuit issue, some wearing sexy bathing suits, others smoking in sexy poses.

But, as powerful as the tobacco industry is, *you can win this battle.* Although Big Tobacco has big bucks on its side, no money can match what you have going for you—*love.* No slick magazine advertisements, no clever billboard ads, no cigarette-smoking movie or TV stars, no tobacco sponsorship of popular sports or musical events can win when matched up against *your love for your child.*

This is not an easy struggle for parents. In our media-saturated society, Big Tobacco comes after kids every way that it can. The tobacco companies have to addict your teenagers to their lethal—but legal—products or they will go out of business. If your teenagers don't replace the adult smokers of today—who are dying from smoking-related diseases—the tobacco industry will find itself in the dustbin of history.

A Life and Death Struggle

You are involved in a life-and-death struggle against Big Tobacco. On the outcome depends the health and happiness of your teenager. Big Tobacco is a formidable foe. The industry has used its great financial resources, not only to learn how to grow more potent plants and to manufacture more addictive products, but also to understand the psychology of human beings to better manipulate them into buying their deadly product. In a sense, the tobacco industry may know more about your teenager than you do. Big Tobacco understands how to appeal to and manipulate teenage psychology.

The tobacco companies have studied the hopes, fears, conflicts, and desires of teenagers so that it can create advertisements that will lure your teen to try their products. They understand that teenagers want to rebel, to be independent, to be their true selves, yet, at the same time, teens want to belong, to fit in, and to be part of the group. The tobacco industry knows what is important to teenagers—love, success, sexuality, accomplishment—and it skillfully links cigarettes to all of these teen desires. The industry also knows what teens fear—not being cool, feeling self-conscious and awkward, failing and not belonging—and offers cigarettes as an answer to those emotional anxieties.

As long as it can exploit the psychological conflicts and insecurities that are a part of adolescence in our society, the tobacco industry knows there will be an initial demand for their product.

To help your teenager quit smoking, it is important to know the facts about tobacco and the harm that smoking causes. But you will need more than facts. You will need to know yourself and to know your teenager. That may sound like a tall order but it doesn't have to be done overnight. *It is a process*. It is a way of life. The foundation for this way of life is honest communication with your children and teenagers. Again, this is easier said than done but it is possible. No one does it perfectly. A parent just has to give it his or her best shot.

Recently, on C-SPAN, a teenager from Virginia told a panel of experts on smoking—an industry spokesman, a senatorial staff member, and an antismoking activist—that "kids are going to smoke no matter what the laws are because they rebel and because it's cool. I think kids need parents to instill in them that they can be comfortable with themselves. I think that's why kids start smoking." The teen makes two important points. The tobacco industry does portray cigarette smoking as an antidote for various forms of discomfort. Adolescence can be a time of great discomfort and this can make smoking seem appealing. Also, the teenager pointed out the important role parents play in relation to teen smoking.

How influential are parents and the home environment when it comes to smoking? A look at attitudes in two states provides a clearer picture. In Kentucky, a state in which tobacco plays a key role in the economy, many adults smoke and smoking is looked upon favorably in general. Kentucky has a high rate of teenage smoking. In contrast, Utah has a low rate of teen smoking. This is because a sizable portion of the population is Mormon and smoking (along with alcohol and caffeine) are forbidden in that religion. These two examples clearly illustrate the power of cultural/religious beliefs and parental behavior to affect teenage smoking.

HEALTH HAZARD TO YOUR TEEN

In 1964—the year of the first Surgeon General's report on the hazards of smoking—50 percent of American men smoked. In 1998, 25 percent of American men are smokers. However, in the early to mid-1960s, to replace the millions of men who were quitting smoking, the tobacco industry targeted young women as its next consumers, or victims. There is about a twenty-year lag between the start of smoking and the appearance of disease, such as cancer. It was no surprise, then, when the lung cancer rates for women began to climb dramatically in the early 1980s. Lung cancer in women has now reached epidemic proportions.

According to the American Cancer Society, 80,100 women were diagnosed with lung cancer in 1998. That same year, 67,000 women died of lung cancer—23,500 more than died of breast cancer. Ninety percent of these women got cancer because they smoked. These statistics involve women who began smoking in the late 1950s and in the 1960s. Your teenage daughters are now being targeted by the tobacco companies. They could be the cancer victims of the early twenty-first century. Teenage girls are now smoking at higher rates than boys. Many studies show that it is more difficult for women to quit smoking than for men. To make matters worse, today's women smoke more heavily than women did years ago.

Teenage girls who begin smoking today are not just at risk of lung cancer. Smoking increases a women's risk of cancers of the esophagus, larynx, bladder, kidney, pancreas, stomach, and cervix. In addition, about 100,000 women die each year from cardiovascular disease that is related to smoking. Women are at risk of having a heart attack or dying of heart disease if they smoke as few as one to four cigarettes a day. Stroke, emphysema, premature wrinkling, early menopause, pregnancy problems (such as miscarriage or stillbirth), and osteoporosis can all result from smoking.

To further compound the problem for women, they seem to be more vulnerable to the effects of tobacco than men. For example, lung cancer is about three times more likely in women who smoke than in men who smoke the same amount. And the lung cancer risk does not go away entirely when a woman quits smoking. About half of women diagnosed with lung cancers had quit the habit years before.

Both teenage boys and girls are the targets of the tobacco industry. Parents need to be aware of the important differences in the effects of smoking on either sex. These will be dealt with later in the book. Smoking, however, cannot be looked at in isolation. You can only help your teenager if you see cigarette-smoking in the context of your teen's whole life.

ADOLESCENCE AND SEXUALITY

For parents and teenagers, adolescence is a time of great change. It is fascinating and frustrating, challenging and confusing, all at once. For each boy or girl, puberty begins at a different age, typically between ages eleven and fifteen. Physical changes in girls usually begin earlier. Breast changes can start between ages ten and eleven. Menarche (or the first period) frequently occurs about eighteen months after these breast changes. For boys, the growth of pubic hair is the first sign of puberty and this can occur from age eleven onward. There is tremendous variation in the timing, and rate of development, of puberty.

Boys and girls have different reactions to puberty. At childhood's end, a youngster finds his or her whole body changing. Complexions change; ears seem to stick out; a nose seems horribly prominent suddenly. Kids are inundated with thousands of media images promoting a certain kind of physical beauty and cannot help but compare how they look with these carefully crafted commercial visions of masculinity and femininity. Exaggerated media images can contribute to painful self-consciousness and lack of self-esteem. Even supermodel

Cindy Crawford once remarked, upon seeing a picture of herself on a fashion magazine cover, "I don't even look like that!" If the models themselves don't live up to their own images, what can an average teen expect? Some studies show that girls as young as five years of age are already negatively affected by media images of female beauty.

Boys and girls also respond differently to the early onset of puberty. For boys, the growth in size and the development of physical strength usually provide a social advantage among their peers. Boys who experience puberty later may go through painful years in which they become shy and insecure.

For girls, early puberty may cause some problems. More than boys, girls compare their bodies with media illusions—and come up short in their minds. Girls don't know that media images are a product of fashion and can change dramatically. For example, Marilyn Monroe—the ultimate beauty queen of her era—would be considered "fat" by today's emaciated standards. Young girls often respond to these media images by trying to lose weight. Studies show that most young girls who diet are at their normal weight or even below normal weight. In contrast, teenage boys more frequently try to gain weight to build up their bodies. Parents need to be aware that girls who experience puberty early on may be prone to a number of psychosocial problems. Research indicates that such girls may be more likely to smoke, drink alcohol, or use drugs. They may also become sexually active at a younger age.

SEXUALITY AND LIFE ENERGY

The essence of puberty is sexual maturation. In our culture, in which adolescent biology and society are frequently at odds, this can be a difficult period for both teens and parents. All parents have strongly held beliefs and values—religious, moral, ethical—that they hope to impart to their children. Parental views on sexuality shape the way their teenagers view sex. But for teenagers, adolescent sexuality is more about physiology and emotional life than about religious, moral, or ethical beliefs.

At the beginning of the twentieth century, Sigmund Freud made a revolutionary discovery about human sexuality. He found that sexuality is with us from birth onward and develops throughout life in a gradually unfolding process. Until Freud, it was believed that sexuality appeared suddenly, as if from nowhere, at puberty. It took over half a century for this view to become widely accepted in Western society. However, surveys conducted in recent years reveal that a sizable proportion of the American public still believes, erroneously, that human sexuality first appears during puberty.

About sixty years ago, Wilhelm Reich, one of Freud's most prominent students, pursued the investigation of human sexuality further. Reich discovered that there is a specific physical bioenergy in human beings that expresses itself in human growth, in work, in creativity, and in human sexuality. Reich moved the study of sexuality beyond psychology to biology. His writings about adolescent sexuality and psychology are valid

and valuable today, more than six decades after they were published.

During adolescence, teens experience powerful surges of
this bioenergy. The spontaneous joy of life; the developing interest in sex; the seemingly boundless energy of youth; the desire
to explore, experiment, and discover—all these are expressions
of the bioenergy, or Life Energy, in your teenager. There are
many bumps in the road for teenagers during this period as they
learn through living to handle their profound emotional, intellectual, and physical changes. Finding equilibrium and balance is no simple task for teens—or anyone else for that matter.

Unfortunately, sex is still a subject that makes many people uncomfortable. It can be particularly difficult for parents
to speak openly with their teens about sex. Schools generally
teach the basics about the anatomy and physiology of sexual
activity—the "plumbing"—and usually promote abstinence
from sexual activity for teenagers. When teens need an adult to
communicate with about the central phenomenon of their lives,
they too often find a grown-up who is anxious and who wants to
avoid the subject. Or they encounter a person with strict, dog-
matic moral or religious views, who is willing to preach to kids
but not to listen to them. On occasion, a teen comes across an adult
who has a tolerant attitude toward teen sexuality. But rarely do
young people find an older person who *affirms* their natural sexuality and tries to help them understand what they are feeling.

Sexuality is a natural expression of the Life Energy in teens,
and parents who are open with their children can help them
become comfortable with who they are; with the changes they

are going through; with the confusion they feel. Patience and a sense of perspective are essential. Parents generally know their children well but when puberty hits, it can seem as if a stranger has moved in to replace their boy or girl.

BIG TOBACCO SELLS SEX

How does all this relate to quitting smoking? It's simple. Big Tobacco is not afraid to deal directly with adolescent sexuality. Big Tobacco exploits teenage sexuality to sell its lethal products. Slick advertising campaigns are based on a thorough study of psychology and a misuse of this knowledge to lure people into buying a harmful product. Big Tobacco knows how to use the confusion and ambivalence of teens to its own advantage.

All a parent needs to do is to look at the cigarette ads themselves for proof. Sexual titillation is obvious in many ads. The cigarette ads in the *Sports Illustrated* "swimsuit" issue are an excellent example of this. In others, the sexual exploitation is a bit more subtle, but it is present nonetheless. Big Tobacco presents powerful positive images of macho men and alluring women—all of which appeal to teens—and links these images with cigarettes. One of the great crimes perpetrated by Big Tobacco is that it manipulates the Life Energy of your teen and redirects it to make its deadly products desirable. Its products become an unconscious substitute for what teens really want in life and an answer to circumstances or situations that make teens feel uncomfortable.

Most of the other topics that follow are directly related to teen sexuality. The tobacco companies exploit every one of them in some way to promote their products. Parents need to be as aware of these subjects as are the cigarette manufacturers.

APPEARANCE AND FASHION

The great physical changes that teens go through in adolescence, and the profound emotional changes associated with their ongoing physical development, make appearance extremely important to most teenagers. Appearance and current teen fads in fashion are one of the most common sources of friction between parents and their children.

If parents from the Baby Boom generation are concerned about their teen's appearance, they need only think back to the sixties and early seventies. How many fathers wore their hair long at that time? How many mothers wore miniskirts? How many parents dressed very casually or colorfully when their parents wanted them to wear attire that was more conventional?

Learning to choose one's battles wisely can ease many of the stresses of life. And the battle over appearance between parents and teens may not be worth it. A parent may be better off taking a stand on more important issues. For the teenager, having the right to choose what to wear is far more important than the clothing or the hairstyle. A parent who looks back at his or her youth will see that the fashions of the day did not do them any irreparable harm. Similarly, allowing their sons and daughters to determine their own appearance usually poses no threat of harm. If the lines of communication are open, and parents show respect for their teens, the few fads that may be unwise or dangerous (tattooing or body-piercing, for example) can be discussed and thought through together. In the area of appearance and fashion, compromise is usually possible.

However, it is a different story with a teenager's physical looks. It can be very damaging for parents—no matter how well-intentioned they may be—to tease kids about looks during this period. A "humorous" comment about an aspect of appearance—the nose, the ears, developing breasts—can be extremely painful. From the earliest ages, children are subjected to a barrage of images of accepted and desired body types and images of what is considered beautiful and handsome that very few of us inherit.

During adolescence, young people are particularly vulnerable to anxieties and concern over their physical looks and their appearance. Parents need to pay attention to teen behavior in this area because serious problems may develop. For example, young girls may develop eating disorders in an attempt to become thin. Boys may experiment with over-the-counter or prescription drugs (e.g., steroids) to help them build up their muscle mass. Parents who listen to their children, and who share with them some of the insecurities and fears they had in their adolescence, can be of great help to their teens at this time.

Big Tobacco is there with its message for your sons and daughters—boys who smoke are macho men; girls who smoke are slim, sexy, and sophisticated. Big Tobacco is ready to exploit the emotional insecurities of youngsters and to offer them the illusory gratification that comes with smoking cigarettes. The nicotine will hook them and keep the teens coming back even when they realize that smoking doesn't help solve their emotional insecurities in any way.

A parent involved in World War III with a teenager over hairstyle, clothing, and other passing fashion fads is less likely to be able to talk to a teen about the deadly potential of smoking or to help a teen quit smoking. Clearly, cigarettes pose more of a threat than hair dyed pink or a skirt an inch too short. Smoking is a crucial place to take a stand because your teen's health and happiness are on the line.

WEIGHT

Weight and appearance are inextricably related. Today, Americans are brainwashed by the fashion industry and by advertisements of all kinds into believing that an emaciated state is the ideal of physical beauty for women. This widespread attitude has an extremely negative impact on both young girls and young boys. Harmful fad diets appear, promise much, fail to deliver, and then vanish from the scene—only to be replaced instantaneously by the newest fad diet. Diet sodas, cakes, cookies, and ice creams and specially formulated diet meals fill the shelves of supermarkets. "No Fat" or "Fat Free" signs are prominent on products everywhere, even on pizza.

Yet, despite this worship of thinness, and the popularity of numerous diets and diet programs, Americans are more over-weight than they have ever been in the nation's history. A seden-tary lifestyle, lack of regular physical exercise, and poor eating habits are primarily to blame. American teenagers are heavier than in years past as well. The definition of overweight keeps changing—a new definition was proposed as this book was being written. However, there is ample evidence that carrying too much weight is detrimental to health. People who are signifi-cantly overweight are at increased risk of developing serious health problems such as heart disease, to name but one.

In our society, being overweight is looked down on and often mocked. Teens who are heavier than their peers are frequently teased and made to feel unwanted. For example, they may not be asked out for dates and they may not be picked for athletic teams. A parent's unconditional love for his or her child is the best medicine here. A youngster is more than a symptom—heavy or overweight. A teenager is a complete human being—body, mind, and spirit—with hopes, dreams, and fears. A parent who talks to his or her teen, who listens, and who empathizes can be of great help.

Once again, your teenager needs you to be there, to share your experience, to offer suggestions and advice. For once again, Big Tobacco is there with its deadly advice and its answer for your son or daughter—*light up a cigarette.* Smoking is pre-sented as an answer to being overweight. Big Tobacco is par-ticularly effective in getting this message across to young women. How about the brand-name *Virginia Slims?* Through powerful magazine ads, young woman are repeatedly shown images of wafer-thin, beautiful models happily smoking away. The message is clear: smoking will keep you thin, and thin is sexy, beautiful, sophisticated, and desirable.

EMOTIONAL DEVELOPMENT

In a song he wrote as a solo artist, John Lennon sang, "Children, do not do what I have done / I couldn't walk and I tried to run." Though the physical changes that teenagers undergo are quite obvious, the equally powerful emotional upheavals they experience may not be so apparent to the busy parent. Teen emotional growth is a more subtle phenomenon but it is critical to your child's health and happiness. Just as an adolescent's body grows in bursts of Life Energy, so too her emotional development grows in unpredictable jumps and starts.

Physical maturity, sexual maturation, and emotional development will most likely not all occur at the same rate. And this can cause a great deal of turmoil for parent and teen alike. In addition, a teenager's intellect is evolving at this time as well. And the cognitive development—honed through life experiences—may not be in sync with emotional growth. A teen's cognitive skills may either lag behind or be far ahead of his or her emotional development.

During adolescence, teens begin to think critically. Unfortunately for parents, they are usually the first targets of this new criticism. But, with a sense of perspective and a sense of humor, most parents can make it through this period relatively unscathed. Intellectual arguments with parents can be quite a boon to teens at this time, helping them to sharpen their intellectual skills and to begin to think clearly and independently.

At this time, teens start to differentiate their viewpoints from those of their parents. This can pose difficulties for parents with strong specific religious, moral, ethical, and cultural beliefs who want their children to accept their values uncritically. Teenagers question as part of their natural development. Many become intensely interested in moral and social values; in how adults apply the beliefs they espouse to the real world—or don't. Many teens are at first shocked by, and then rebel against, what they perceive as the hypocrisy of the adult world. (And there certainly is a lot of adult hypocrisy in evidence.)

Although teens may challenge parental authority and beliefs during adolescence, most research shows that teenagers usually accept and uphold the values that their parents imparted to them. A parent who has perspective—and essentially trusts his or her teen—can more easily make it through this period of challenging and questioning parental authority.

TEEN INDEPENDENCE

As teenagers become more independent, friends begin to become more important than family. This may also be difficult for parents to accept. Separating from parents is necessary. Teens are not so much rejecting their families as they are building their own lives. It is essential that teens develop friendships away from home and learn who to trust and who to love and how to interact with peers. It is in this way that a teenager becomes her true self.

Parents know that they separated from their own families—but that did not mean, usually, that they severed relations with their parents. Teens and parents will reunite once again, on a more firm foundation, after a teen finds her own life and self. Again, open, honest, ongoing communication is crucial.

During this period, teens need to be able to turn to their parents for advice and support. They will make mistakes and choose friends who turn out not to be good for them. Teens will make the mistakes we all make and have made. Parents who can share parts of their own growing-up with their children can do untold good. The transition away from family to new friends can be awkward for both teens and parents and there will be difficult situations when desires, expectations, and hopes clash. Acknowledging different needs openly—and respecting them equally—can help parents and teens to create solutions together.

Strong contact between parents and teens is invaluable as the adolescent sets out "to find" himself, since powerful cigarette ads abound urging him to try smoking as an answer to the confusion and stress of everyday teen life. The omnipresent images of secure, confident smokers call out to kids: "Worried or stressed out? Just light up!" "Self-conscious? Have a smoke!" "Disappointed? A cigarette will fix that!"

Big Tobacco is amoral and has no qualms about exploiting the most vulnerable aspects of your teenager's emerging personality. Big Tobacco has done its homework and knows just how to get young people to try their addictive product. But you can be there for your son or daughter and help to diminish the impact of alluring media images.

DEPRESSION

Depression is extremely common and affects 8 to 15 percent of Americans at some time in their lives. Yet depression is widely overlooked, misdiagnosed, and mistreated by the medical profession. Although it has been recognized since ancient times, the exact causes of depression are unknown. Today, it is believed that "biochemical imbalances" play a role in depression. There is also evidence that suggests there is a "genetic" component to depression as well. Sometimes, an undiagnosed, underlying physical illness may be the cause of the depression. The link between the lack of sexual gratification in adolescence and depression is not yet widely appreciated. Serious depression is more easily recognized than mild to moderate depression, which is often dismissed as just part of life or a passing case of "the blues."

If your teenager continually exhibits four or more of the following symptoms of depression for more than two weeks, he or she may be suffering from depression:

- Overwhelming feelings of sadness or grief, with depressed mood.
- Loss of interest in activities usually enjoyed.

- ☐ Sleep disturbances (e.g., insomnia; too much sleep; early morning waking).

- ☐ Fatigue or decreased energy.

- ☐ Significant weight loss or gain; noticeable change in appetite.

- ☐ Feelings of worthlessness, helplessness, guilt.

- ☐ Inability to concentrate.

- ☐ Physical symptoms of restlessness or sluggishness.

- ☐ Recurrent thoughts of death or suicide.

The American Psychiatric Association uses the above as criteria to help diagnose depression. In mild cases, the symptoms are not severe. In severe cases, the symptoms clearly interfere with daily life. In such cases, it may be difficult for your teen to get out of bed in the morning; to go to class; to concentrate and do homework; to see friends and engage in social activities. Teens who are suffering depression may also begin to neglect their appearance.

Although most depression occurs from ages twenty to thirty, it can be present during the teen years. Teen suicide may be a tragic result of undiagnosed and untreated depression. Fortunately, most depressions respond well to treatment. In about 80 percent of cases, the correct diagnosis and treatment leads to improvement and complete remission.

Public misunderstanding of depression, however, can prevent effective treatment of this condition. For example, a survey sponsored by the National Mental Health Association showed that 54 percent of those questioned believed that depression is a sign of "weakness." About one-third of the respondents said they would be too ashamed to seek help. Parents with such misconceptions may not see the warning signs in their teens.

A 1994 study showed that people who are overweight may be more prone to depression—and that *dieting*, not the extra pounds, was causing the depression. Teens who are dieting—especially teenage girls—so that they may be fashionably thin may begin to suffer from depression as a result of their eating patterns.

In addition, sexual frustration and confusion about sexuality may contribute to depression in teenagers. Although sexual maturation is the essence of the biology and physiology of adolescence, our society and culture do not know how to handle this reality satisfactorily. Telling teens to "just say no" when it comes to sex is futile. Preaching abstinence may make adults feel better, but it is no answer. Teen sexuality is a problem our society has been evading and avoiding for most of its history. Although teen sexuality is exploited for commercial gain—by the fashion, cosmetic, and music industries, for example—it is difficult to find an adult who will deal openly and honestly with the essential conflict of teen sexuality: the conflict between the natural sexual desires and needs of the teenager and the sexual fears and prohibitions of the larger society.

The longing and healthy need for physical love on the part of teenagers is a problem for our society. And the lack of gratification teens feel—even among many who are sexually active—contributes to the emotional and psychological problems teens experience, such as depression.

The tobacco advertisements, though, are there with a ready-made solution. "Feeling blue? Angry and frustrated by a world that doesn't understand you? Light up a cigarette, sit back, and blow your blues away." The tough loner with the cigarette is an appealing, romantic image for many. The slim, sexy, and sophisticated woman, looking cool and above it all holding her cigarette, is equally appealing to many young women.

Parents who remember their own transition during adolescence, and who can identify with and understand what their teens are going through, will be better able to help their sons and daughters resist the seductive images of smoking as a way to handle difficult emotional situations.

EMBARRASSMENT AND SHYNESS

Is there a parent alive who did not feel, at some time or another during adolescence, the excruciating self-consciousness and embarrassment that plagues most teenagers at some point in their development? Or the shyness that is related to self-consciousness?

One survey revealed that by junior high school, 50 percent of boys and 60 percent of girls have experienced regular bouts of shyness. Older teens and young adults experience this as well: about 44 percent of eighteen to twenty-one year-olds experience shyness. Many times, shy teens are hypercritical of themselves, which worsens the situation.

Teens have a wide range of reasons for feeling awkward,

shy, and self-conscious. Some reasons are external, others internal; some are superficial and passing, others profound and lasting. For a time, some teens are acutely aware of their changing looks and may be shy around the opposite sex. Other teens may begin to realize that they are attracted to members of the same sex and they do not know how to handle this difficult realization. They may fear the reaction of parents and friends. Society is somewhat more open than in past years, but homosexuality is still considered in a negative light overall. Embarrassment is a problem for most teenagers at some time in life.

At a certain point in their lives, many teens become embarrassed, not by themselves or their innermost feelings, but by their parents. Teens still need their parents, but they also need to separate from their parents and establish their independence. On some occasions, they need to show their independence from the family in front of their friends. Parents may feel hurt at times as their children distance themselves from them. However, this is a phase of development that is necessary. If handled with mutual respect, and a sense of proportion, it will pass.

Not missing a beat, Big Tobacco offers a cigarette in the hand as the way to ward off the discomfort and embarrassment that many teens feel. Cigarette smokers are "cool" and unflappable. They are suave and comfortable around the opposite sex. Cigarette smokers are independent—or so the ads would have teens believe. Parents who have good rapport with their teens can help them see how Big Tobacco is exploiting their emotions to get them to smoke, knowing full well that nicotine addiction will keep them smoking from then on.

PEER PRESSURE

Many parents use the term "peer pressure" only in regard to negative situations. They imagine that their teens will begin to associate with "bad kids" who will influence and pressure their children into taking up unhealthy habits such as cigarette smoking. According to teens themselves, peer pressure is often overrated by adults. And the effects of "bad" kids is exaggerated as well. Most teens are attracted to other kids who share their interests and who enjoy the same activities. In these instances, "peer pressure" is a positive force. Sometimes "good" kids can even exert a positive influence on so-called "bad" kids.

Teens often attack conformity, and assert that they don't want to be like everybody else, but they do have a strong need to *belong*. When parents are uncomfortable with new friends their son or daughter is making, criticizing those friends or trying to prevent the teen from seeing them may backfire big-time. Such parental behavior may force the teenager to defend his or her choice of friends and deepen the bonds that connect them. Many times, parents worry excessively. Teens usually recognize truly "bad" friends on their own and the relationships are short-lived.

As with questions of appearance and dress, parents have to know which battles to choose. Are the friends of their teens truly a danger or do they just irritate the parent for one reason or another? Truly risky behavior—underage drinking; drinking and driving; smoking; drug use; unsafe sex—all require that a parent be a parent. If your teen becomes excessively secretive or unwilling to talk about certain friends and what they do, there may be cause for concern. But garden-variety teenage rebellion is part of life and usually nothing to be overly concerned about.

Big Tobacco tries to connect its products with the desire to belong, to be part of the "in crowd," to be a winner and not a loser. A teen who can turn to her parent, who has an ongoing relationship in which feelings can be discussed, is less likely to take up smoking to spite a disapproving parent, or to be part of a crowd that engages in self-destructive behavior such as smoking. Parents can help their teens by focusing on behaviors and not on friends. Parents need to respect their teens ability to make friends—and their capacity to learn to end friendships with peers who are not good for them.

POPULARITY AND DATING

It isn't just teens who worry about popularity. Too many parents worry about whether their children are popular as well. During adolescence, it is important that teens learn to distinguish "being popular" from having friends. Popularity comes and goes but the ability to make friends, and to be a friend, is critical to happiness and fulfillment in life.

Studies show that the average teen and the most popular teens all do reasonably well in life. However, it is those who are *rejected* during their teens—either by their peers or their parents—

who frequently have serious trouble later in life. Teens may be rejected because of their own inappropriate behavior, poor social skills, or simply because they are so different from their peers that they are not understood. Whatever the reasons for rejection may be, it is a reality that parents need to be aware of.

Popularity and dating are closely related. Although parents want their teens to be popular and to date, it is precisely dating that causes the most concern and friction between parents and teens. Parents wonder if their teens are "ready" to date. There is great variation among teens in this area. In general, girls are ready to date at an earlier age than boys. Of course, this causes much anxiety since many parents are more protective of their daughters than of their sons. Dating is difficult for many teens as well. They are taking the first tentative steps toward building more complex relationships with others. The potential for emotional intimacy can be intimidating for teens. The potential for sexual intimacy is usually what most worries parents.

As difficult as it may be, it is important that parents don't panic when their teens announce they are "going steady." It is equally important not to panic if your teen doesn't seem interested in dating when many of his or her peers are beginning to date. Parents who have made communication an important part of their relationship with their children have less to worry about. They can talk to their teens about *feelings*. If you ask your teenager how he or she is feeling—and if you listen to his or her answer—you will be able to provide much-needed support for their first forays into the wide world of relationships.

Dating is integral to growing up, to maturing. Unfortunately, teens (and even preteens) are subjected to great pressures and inappropriate messages from movies, TV, and music videos. The mass media exploits adolescent sexuality for its own commercial gain and gives kids distorted images of sexuality and erroneous ideas about how to interact with the opposite sex. While our culture promotes abstinence for teens in its churches and schools, it shamelessly titillates and exploits teens with sexually provocative images. Adult society is giving teens a profoundly mixed message.

The individual teenager's level of maturity—not a chronological age—is the most important factor in whether or not a teen is "ready" to date. An emotionally immature teenager is more likely to drink alcohol, smoke cigarettes, use drugs, and engage in high-risk sexual activity. This is where kids need their parents. Teens need parents who will help guide them, who will support their healthy, positive development, and who will point out dangerous illusions that can cause them harm.

Big Tobacco has illusions galore to offer as answers to shyness and low self-esteem that can follow rejection; to the pain and loneliness the rejected teen may feel. According to all the cigarette ads, there's no problem that a smoke won't solve. A teen who feels cut off and isolated is more susceptible to the false promise of relief from uncomfortable feelings that smoking promises to bring. A young girl who feels unattractive can assume a glamorous pose simply by smoking the right brand of cigarette. A boy who wants to be more masculine to attract girls can do so by lighting up. You can be there for your teenager and offer an alternative view to that of high-impact cigarette advertising. If you have been honest with your teen, he will be more likely to believe you than Big Tobacco.

ALCOHOL

Of all the legal drugs, alcohol may be the most destructive. The facts about alcohol use among youngsters may shock some parents. A 1992 survey found that 70 percent of eighth-graders had used alcohol. And 27 percent of eighth-graders had gotten drunk. In high schools all around the country, many teens consider drinking to be part of growing up. It is estimated that 40 percent of boys in high school binge drink (that is, have five or more drinks at one time). It is almost a rite of passage. About 80 percent of male college freshmen and 70 percent of first-year female college students drink alcohol. Nearly one-third of the women and half of the men say they get drunk regularly. Parents worry about illegal drug use but drinking causes far greater problems and threats to their teens. Heroin, crack, and cocaine—these are the "hard drugs" that spook parents. These are the targets of a twenty-year-long failed War on Drugs that has been waged by the Federal government and that has cost untold billions of dollars. Each year, 2,400 people die from using heroin and morphine. And each year, about 3,300 die from using crack and cocaine. In contrast, 105,000 people die each year as a result of drinking alcohol.

Alcohol poses a perplexing problems for parents because

it is legal, widely used, and accepted by society. There may be additional problems for many parents who drink alcohol. There are no easy answers. Many parents who drank and perhaps experimented with drugs in the sixties and seventies when they were young have an especially difficult time talking to their teenagers about these topics. The situation as we enter the twenty-first century is far different from what it was thirty to forty years ago. We know so much more about the hazards of smoking, drinking alcohol, and taking drugs than we did at that time. Therefore, it may be possible for parents who drank as teens, and who may still drink alcohol, as well as parents who have quit, to talk to their teens realistically about the hazards of drinking.

THE ALLURE OF SMOKING: FROM TEENS TO NICO-TEENS

There is an important link between drinking and smoking, especially at an early age. Frequently, drinking leads to cigarette smoking. In 1992, a survey revealed that 45 percent of eighth-graders had experimented with smoking cigarettes. It is known that this is the age at which most confirmed smokers begin. And 21 percent had tried smokeless tobacco. The same study revealed that seven out of ten eighth-graders also had experimented with alcohol. In contrast, only 11 percent had tried marijuana or hashish. Youngsters have relatively easy access to our legal drugs—alcohol and tobacco—and are using them at early ages.

The majority of teenagers experiment with alcohol, tobacco, and illegal drugs. But most of them do not become addicted. However, of those teens who do become addicted to drugs, the vast majority fall prey to the highly advertised, socially acceptable drugs—alcohol and tobacco—and not to so-called "hard drugs."

Teens are more likely to smoke if a parent or family member smokes. White teenagers are more likely to smoke than black teens, although smoking by black teens is on the rise. Teens who do not plan to continue school after high school are also more than twice as likely to smoke cigarettes than those who plan to attend college or junior college. School policies also affect teen smoking. One survey showed that schools that allow or tolerate teen smoking have 25 percent more smokers than schools that do not allow teen smoking.

Boys and girls smoke in about the same numbers today. However, this indicates that young girls are smoking in far greater numbers than in past years. In the 1960s, Big Tobacco devised ad campaigns that targeted women. They were highly successful. Lung cancer death rates for women now far exceed the mortality rates for breast cancer. Yet, our society tolerates the marketing of this deadly product to its young girls. Your daughter's life means less to Big Tobacco than the money she will spend during her lifetime buying cigarettes.

In general, boys begin smoking to assert their masculinity. The images of the macho male smoker influence some young boys to begin smoking. Many boys also begin to smoke in order to be part of a group they want to belong to because it is important to their self-image. The nicotine addiction they develop keeps them coming back. In the 1970s, there was a Top 40 hit song, "Smokin' in the Boys Room." The tune seemed to be about teenage rebellion at high school. Actually, the phenomenon of boys—and girls—sneaking off to the bathroom for a smoke between classes has far more to do with nicotine addiction than with rebellion. Kids who have to light up aren't rebels; they are slaves to nicotine who are experiencing *withdrawal.*

Frequently, girls are enticed to smoke by images of slim, sexy, sophisticated women. In addition, many girls in our society have been inculcated with distorted images of their bodies through the mass media and use cigarettes as a means of weight control. The fact that smoking is of no real help in controlling weight does not get through to teens. And when young girls are addicted, the facts do not even really matter. As with teen boys, the powerful nicotine addiction keeps them smoking.

Unfortunately, it is more difficult to reach teenagers than adults with the facts about the hazards of smoking. Adults are more open to information about not starting or quitting smoking. The warnings on the cigarette packs have no influence on teens. Recent data suggest that large increases in the cost of a pack of cigarettes deter adults more than teens as well. Most teens feel invulnerable and live for the moment. Distant threats of illness and death mean far less than the immediate gratification of lighting up. Add adolescent rebelliousness to the mix and you only magnify the problem.

Big Tobacco has the same facts about your teenagers that you do. In addition, Big Tobacco has billions of dollars and thousands of people—scientists, psychologists, advertising and marketing specialists, public relations professionals, and well-connected lobbyists—working day and night to promote their deadly products. Over 420,000 people a year die as a result of smoking in the United States each year. They die as a result of using a legal product as it is intended to be used. If a company tried to introduce tobacco today as a new product, it would not be allowed to do so. It would be illegal. When a pharmaceutical company introduces a drug that kills or injures people, there is a national uproar. But Big Tobacco is different; the leaders of the tobacco industry can even lie to Congress under oath with impunity. It is that powerful.

You are interested in helping your children become happy and healthy adults. Big Tobacco is interested only in making vast amounts of money by turning your beautiful sons and daughters from teens into *nico-teens*. But you can beat Big Tobacco. It will be a challenge. It won't be easy by any means. But you can help your teen quit smoking if you develop a relationship with your teen based on open, honest communication and empathy.

Life is constant change and adventure for a teenager. Teens are doing everything for the first time. That is the agony and the ecstasy of adolescence. The first love and the first loss of love occur so close in time. Happiness and sorrow; success and failure; hope and disappointment all follow in rapid succession in school, at home, and with new friends. Teens experience great exhilaration and great stress. Big Tobacco tries to exploit the emotional turmoil of teens to addict them. With love and compassion, you can support your son or daughter in a successful struggle to escape from nicotine addiction.

COMMUNICATION

The whole tone of parent-child communication changes during adolescence. Teens are naturally beginning to assert themselves. The young children who generally listened to and obeyed their parents are now replaced by teens who question, argue with, and even defy parents. Classic battles develop over many issues as teen desires conflict with parental wishes. An emerging teen autonomy clashes with long-standing adult authority.

During adolescence, teenagers begin to see a reality that may be unsettling and unflattering to many parents. Teens become aware that their parents aren't perfect. They become aware that their parents don't know everything and that they aren't always right. As they mature, teenagers become aware that their parents are *people*.

Although this change in parent-child relations can be disturbing, it is also necessary for the healthy development of young people. Teenagers need to learn how to assert themselves. And they need to be able to make mistakes in the process. Our errors are often our best teachers. Reasonable differences of opinion between parents and teens can result in a healthy conflict that brings positive results. In fact, parents who are aware of the change that is taking place in their relations with their children can learn as much from the challenging interactions with their teens as the youngsters themselves.

Arguments can be repetitive, frustrating, and even infuriating at times. However, if a parent can see that this bumpy part of the road is leading toward a time when their sons and daughters will be better able to take care of themselves, it may be less stressful. Productive arguments can help teens learn to think

A TEEN'S MESSAGE TO TEENS

"I need to know that my mother and father are standing by me," said a fifteen-year old girl "or I have no one." This thoughtful, articulate teen agreed to be interviewed for this book on the condition of complete confidentiality.

"Kids often complain that 'my parents don't understand me.' I think that parents really do understand. But many parents have to work too hard. My mom worked a nine-to-five job, came home and worked in the house, and then went to school at night. But both of my parents showed me love, kindness, and patience. My dad sits down and talks to me. He really listens. My parents give me the help I need. My parents listen to me but they also give me guidance."

This teen was raised by parents who imparted their values to her. They also spoke to her about smoking, providing her with the facts. "My parents taught me important facts for themselves. However, excessive conflict and problems that remain unresolved over prolonged periods of time may require outside help. Counseling for the teen, the parents, or all parties may be extremely valuable.

Honest communication between adults and teens is the key to getting through this potentially difficult time. Communication involves more than parents telling teens what to do. More

about smoking," she said. "For example, they told me that it is harder for women to quit smoking than for men. I believe my parents because they talk openly with me about their life experiences. They have always been there for me. Why shouldn't I believe them?"

She acknowledged that many teens don't listen to their parents and smoke out of rebellious emotions. "Parents need to be parents," she insisted, but noted that "sometimes parents don't see what their kids really need. They need love."

This young teen doesn't smoke and has never smoked. "My parents encouraged me to *be myself*. To ask myself if I think it's okay to smoke. They encouraged me to ask myself *why* I was thinking of smoking and to think about how smoking would affect me. My parents taught me to listen to myself."

of the burden of success falls on the parents because they have lived longer, have more experience, and—hopefully—are more mature than their teens. Perspective is also critical to communication. If a parent can keep his or her perspective, and see that some arguments are a part of normal life with teens, it diminishes the intensity of the battle of wills. Parents can step back and review the situation. Is the argument really about what the teen wishes to do? Or is the argument a result of a parental desire to maintain control or power? A parent can pause a moment to reflect during an argument, to listen to what the teenager is saying, and consider it seriously. The parent can look at his own actions and words to see what role he is playing in the argument.

A parent can often help resolve conflicts with their kids by listening and by asking the teen to help solve the problem. A mature adult can step back from the battle of wills and ask the teen to come up with a plan that is satisfactory to both sides. In this way, the parent shows respect for the teen and the youngster learns to think things through and to see that conflicts can be resolved through cooperation.

Ongoing, open, direct communication between parents and children is essential if parents are to help their teens successfully resist the powerful illusory lures of Big Tobacco. The cigarette manufacturers, through their ads, offer visions of independence to teenagers. And teens struggling with their parents for independence can be caught in the cigarette manufacturers' traps, if they feel they are losing the battle for independence. Too often, teens feel their parents don't listen to them;

don't understand them and their needs; don't allow them the freedom to explore life in their own way.

If a teen feels frustrated and misunderstood, and the lines of communication aren't open, the teen may begin to smoke as an ineffective form of rebellion and protest. However, if parents and teens are engaged in an ongoing dialogue, there is a great possibility that teen smoking can be prevented. And, even if a teen tries smoking as an experiment, the parent that has an established, healthy way of talking *and listening* to the teen has a better chance of helping the teen to limit the length of the period of smoking.

CHAPTER TWO
What Teens Need to Know

Teens need to know the facts about smoking. There is no need to exaggerate the dangers of cigarettes and other tobacco products because the reality itself is so bad. The truth about smoking will keep many kids from picking up the habit. Teens who have started smoking and who want to quit need to learn coping strategies to help them stop. These are the hard facts teens need to know to quit smoking. But teenagers need more than just the facts about cigarette smoking to be able to quit.

They need to know about themselves. They need to learn about who they are and what they are going through physically, emotionally, and mentally. In Joseph Heller's great novel, *Catch 22*, Heller writes that one of his characters "didn't know what a pariah was, but he knew what it was like to feel like one." Similarly, teens do not know what an "adolescent" is, or what "adolescence" is, but all teens know what it feels like to be one.

Teens need their parents to help them learn who they are.

WHAT IS ADOLESCENCE?

The word *adolescent* comes from the Latin word *adolescere* meaning "to grow up." It has been used in the English language since the fifteenth century, although its exact meaning has varied throughout human history, from era to era, and from one culture to another. In prehistoric times, it is likely that once boys and girls achieved physical maturity they assumed adult roles. In Sumerian society, which flourished from about 5000–2000 B.C.E., parent-teen relations seem to have evolved to a point most parents could recognize today. Scholars have translated a conversation between a Sumerian father and son from about 2,500 years ago, which, roughly translated, is as follows: "Where are you going?" the father asked. "Out," the teen replied. "You have time to go out but not to do your school work?"

Sound familiar? By the time of Plato and Aristotle, adolescence was seen as a time of transition, in which youth would learn a great deal that would prepare them to be responsible adults. In Europe, in the Middle Ages, teens were viewed as basically nothing other than miniature adults. By the Renaissance, it was thought that the "savage" in children was tamed as adolescents were taught to become "rational" beings.

In the United States, in 1800, the average age of the early American population was only sixteen. Life expectancy was short and teenagers, both boys and girls, assumed adult responsibilities. They worked long and hard simply to survive. In the early twentieth century, our picture of adolescence began to change as knowledge of other cultures became more widely known to people in the West. For example, the anthropologist Margaret Mead studied adolescents in Samoa and concluded that much of the stress and turmoil our teens endure is caused by society and not biology. In other cultures, such as described by the pioneering anthropologist Malinowski, social mores and adolescent development, especially sexual development, were in harmony and not at odds as they are in our culture.

Today, in the United States and most other developed nations, adolescence begins earlier and ends later than in the past. Improved nutrition and higher economic standards are primarily responsible for this situation. One of the major challenges a teenager faces is establishing his or her autonomy; that is, emotional and economic independence from the parents. This is a process that begins anywhere from age twelve to fifteen. By around age fifteen, the teen's peer group begins to become more important than his family. Although this can cause some conflict and friction, it is a natural part of development.

TEENS LEARN TO CREATE THEIR LIVES

Adolescent psychosocial and psychosexual development can be broken down into four broad categories. In each category, teens are learning how to create their own lives through experience. In the process of trial and error, there will be many errors. Parents who are there for their kids, who share their life experience with their teens, can help minimize the impact of mistakes. But errors cannot be eliminated; they are an essential part of learning.

During adolescence, teens learn to accept the physical changes that they are undergoing. Their physical growth and development cause great stress and confusion at times, but also bring joy and excitement as well. Teens are also learning to establish peer relationships, independent of parents and siblings. They are beginning to learn who they are, what they believe, and how to be true to themselves. During this period, friends are made and lost; "puppy love" prospers and fades; and friendships begin to develop that will help shape teenagers' identities.

Adolescence is the period in which teens learn how to behave responsibly. Unfortunately for parents, teachers, and other adult authority figures, this does not mean that they always do so. However, the mistakes teens make along the way are essential to this stage of development. Parents who are able to speak openly with their teens can help greatly as their sons and daughters find their way in life.

And teenagers are in a constant process of evolution regarding their personal value system. A teen's values are initially shaped by the parents. The parents' core beliefs are the foundation the teen stands on and from which he or she evaluates the wide range of values and beliefs held by others. Teenagers develop their own values through their experiences with peers and adults. Through this ongoing process, teens develop what experts call a "capacity for future orientation." In other words, they learn to understand the long-term consequences of immediate decisions and behaviors.

In adolescence, biology, psychology, sociology, religion, morality, and ethics are all inextricably interwoven. It is the teenager's task to unravel this tangled web in order to find herself. Parents can help their teens find out who they are. Teens need their parents to help them.

Teenagers need—and deserve—*clear* information from their parents. Even if conversation is at first awkward, it will be effective if it is direct, honest, and sincere. Teenagers need their parents to guide them, to help them make decisions, and to learn to act responsibly. Teens want to take responsibility for their own lives; they just need a helping hand. Scolding or talking down to teens does not work at all. Treating teens with respect works more often than not. Parents who take their teenagers seriously—whether their children come to them worried about acne, school, sex, or smoking—can have a positive impact.

TEENS AND RISK-TAKING

During adolescence, when authority is shifting away from the parents and to the teen, *sharing responsibility* for decisions really works. Parents and teens who can work on life problems together usually succeed in solving them. Of course, this all sounds fine ideally but how does it work in the real world? Risky behavior puts all good intentions to the test.

In a way, it is a teenager's job to take risks. Teens need to stretch out, to spread their wings, to test the limits. Searching and exploring are essential ingredients to a healthy adolescence. The question isn't whether or not teens should take risks. The decision for parents is not to find a way to prevent their children from taking risks. Instead, parents and teens need to focus on *what kind of risks to take.*

Teens are told that drinking and driving is risky behavior. That using illicit drugs or smoking is risky behavior. And they are told that teen sexual activity is risky behavior. Yet, all of these are not truly comparable. Drinking and driving is certainly life-threatening. Thousands of teens die, and tens of thousands are injured, in automobile accidents in which alcohol is involved. The dangers from drugs and smoking cigarettes are also well-known. But sexuality is a central experience of life. Sexual love provides some of the most pleasurable and beautiful experiences in life. It is not clear thinking to lump them all together. Teens need clear thinking.

Parents can help by emphasizing the *positive risks* that teenagers can take. Parents can present their teens with choices. Parents can encourage their teens to try out for one of the school sports teams, to keep them from hanging around with kids who smoke pot. Or suggest that they join the drama club and seek a spot in the cast of the school play. Teens can be encouraged to learn to play an instrument and form a band. Or they can be given a blank book for a present and encouraged to begin to write a journal of their deepest thoughts and feelings.

In addition, teens need to learn the consequences—both immediate and long-term—of negative risks that they may be taking. It is during adolescence that teens are beginning to learn to make the cause-and-effect connections between behavior and its consequences. They need parents to help them do this successfully. And by sharing what they have experienced and learned, parents can help.

The immediate effects of behavior, rather than the long-term, may have more of an impact on teenagers, especially younger teens. When discussing smoking, warning a teen about the occurrence of lung cancer twenty, thirty, or forty years down the road will probably not mean as much as describing the immediate effects: the bad breath, yellow teeth, and stink of cigarette smoke that will become a part of the teen smoker's life.

Some teens are more prone to negative risky behavior than others. Experts have identified some factors that play a role in such behavior by teenagers:

- Early onset of puberty.
- A major life change, such as parental separation or divorce or relocation to a new part of the country.
- Gender (boys are more likely to take negative risks).
- Serious difficulty in the home.
- Mood disorders (e.g., anxiety, depression) and alienation.
- Physical and/or sexual abuse.

In a sense, risky behavior is an inappropriate and ineffective way in which teens seek to handle the stress and strain of difficult life situations and emotions that trouble them deeply.

TEENS AND PREVENTION

As with so much in life, *prevention* is much more effective. Parents who understand what their teens are going through will have a better chance in helping them. All the evidence to date indicates that teens who have grown up in a home in which parents set reasonable and consistent rules do better in life. In addition, teens who have been able to talk openly to their parents since their early years are less likely to engage in negative risky behavior. Because they have been able to talk freely in the past, teens are more likely to discuss their concerns about sex, dating, drugs and alcohol, and smoking with their parents. And teens whose parents listen to them are more likely to listen to their parents.

A TEEN'S MESSAGE TO TEENS

A fifteen-year-old girl interviewed for this book shared some thoughts that relate not only to stopping smoking, but also to many other aspects of life. Her remarks are relevant to both teenagers and adults.

"*Be yourself.* Be a leader, not a follower. Who do you hang out with? Just because your friends smoke, you don't have to smoke. You don't have to change for others. If your friends all jumped off a bridge, would you? Don't be afraid to be yourself, even if it means being alone. Everyone wants to avoid loneliness, but being alone is not the same thing as being lonely. When you are alone, you can focus and you can think clearly. Sometimes you need to be alone. I am a writer and I need to be alone to do my work. But I know that it's okay to be alone, to be quiet, to be with yourself.

"You can ask yourself, 'What am I doing? Why am I smoking? How is this going to affect me?' *Listen to yourself.* My parents taught me to listen to myself."

Often, prevention of risky behavior involves nothing more complicated that a parent helping a teenager *think things through*. A parent who is clear about his or her own views, and who has the knowledge, experience, and information to support those views, can help a teenager understand the implications of such choices as starting to smoke cigarettes. A parent who can teach a teen how to think things through, to see the consequences of behavior, provides an invaluable tool for living.

Parents may need to look at what they do, as well as what they say. A family history of smoking, drinking, or other risky behavior is a strong predictor that teens will engage in similar behavior. Teens need clarity and parents sometimes send mixed messages without knowing it. It is more difficult—but not impossible—for a parent who smokes or drinks to talk to a teen about not picking up the habit. And "boomer" parents who reminisce fondly about their pot-smoking days may undermine their message as well. But parents who are honest about their own smoking or drinking, about the changes their attitudes toward smoking, drugs, and drinking have gone through, can earn the trust of their teens.

WHY TEENS THINK THEY SMOKE

As much as you can do to help your teenager, it is often the case that other teens can exert more of an influence on your son or daughter. Peer pressure, especially in early adolescence, can be very powerful. And teens who have close friends who smoke are at greater risk of smoking than teens whose friends do not smoke. The bad news is that one of every eight teenagers smokes regularly. The good news is that seven of eight teens do not smoke. Since teens listen to other teens, it can be helpful for parents to listen to what teens say about smoking.

Why do teens smoke? When asked, they provide a variety of responses, such as:

- "It helps me relax."
- "All my friends do it."
- "I like it."
- "It keeps my weight down."
- "It helps when I feel stressed out."
- "It made me feel more comfortable at parties and things."
- "It helped me meet other kids. I'd say, 'Like a smoke?' and we'd start to talk."
- "I smoke when I feel down and it helps."
- "Smoking helps me concentrate."

During the interviews with teens conducted for this book, not one of the teens who was presently smoking said, "I'm addicted to cigarettes." All of their reasons for smoking showed that, in their minds, smoking was a way to cope with uncomfortable or difficult situations. The teenagers could not separate why they started smoking from why they continued smoking. Neither could they see that smoking did not really help them stay slim, concentrate, beat the blues, or relieve stress. And almost 100 percent of the teens claimed, "I can stop smoking any time I want." The fact that all but one of them had been smoking from age ten or eleven onward did not seem to contradict their assertions that they could quit smoking whenever they felt like it.

These same teens were asked to give examples of information about smoking that had reached them, and other teens, and made them want to quit. A group of teens were asked what kind of information adults should provide teens about smoking. Again, they provided a wide spectrum of answers, among them:

- Show a picture of a smoker's lungs next to a nonsmoker's lungs.
- Explain how smoking wrinkles your skin.
- Expose how cigarette ads manipulate kids.
- Tell what's really in cigarettes—some have fiberglass; some tobacco is grown with nuclear waste in the fertilizer.
- Show how ads about smoking are all phony.
- Tell teens facts like "Each cigarette takes 14 minutes off your life."
- Add up how much smoking costs—$1,500 a year— and show teens what else they could do with that money.
- Have athletes and TV or movie stars who don't smoke talk to kids.
- Show how smoking interferes with doing what you really want to do, like playing soccer, running, swimming, or just having fun.

- Give all the details about the effects of cigarettes on health.
- Explain to girls that cigarettes don't keep you thin.
- "Show how smoking turns girls off."
- "Show how smoking turns boys off."

As these comments illustrate clearly, there is no one way to reach each individual teenager. That's why it's so important for every parent to know her child. Some kids may see the picture of a smoker's lung (which looks like a burned rubber tire) and never pick up another cigarette. However, another teen may be so scared by the photograph that she runs right out and has a smoke. Most teens hate phoniness and resent it when adults try to manipulate them. These teens may respond to creative dissection of cigarette ads. Many teens are devoted fans of sports stars, movie and TV actors, or pop musicians and would listen to anti-smoking messages from them. Other teens would be oblivious. Health information may change one teen's life while turning another right off. As one young woman said, "Don't try to scare us with a lot of big medical words, like emphysema."

Changing the laws to make it more difficult for teens to get cigarettes, or raising the price of a pack of cigarettes, may not do much to deter teens from smoking. One teen said, "We can get cigarettes any time we want. We buy 'loosies,' individual cigarettes at the corner store." A teenager interviewed on C-SPAN recently observed, "Adults say nicotine is more addictive than heroin. If that's true, price rises and restrictions won't help. Cigarettes in Europe are more expensive than here and many people smoke. The cost of illegal drugs is much higher than cigarettes, yet teens use them."

In general, the teenagers interviewed did not support a ban on cigarettes and tobacco products. However, a number of them thought cigarette and tobacco advertising should be banned. Many teens expressed the view that, in our society, kids are going to smoke because it is cool; that it seems like the adult thing to do; or because they want to rebel against their parents. One teen interviewed on C-SPAN made a suggestion parents

DID YOU KNOW . . .

- Big Tobacco spends more money promoting cigarettes in twenty minutes than is spent in an entire year on smoking prevention?
- The Surgeon General has concluded that cigarette advertising increases teen smoking?
- Marlboro was once a "women's cigarette," advertised as being "As mild as May"?
- The U.S. Armed Forces continued to supply soldiers, sailors, and pilots with cigarettes until 1975, thirteen years after the first Surgeon General's report on the dangers of smoking?
- The Marlboro Man died of lung cancer in 1992 at the age of fifty-one?
- The FDA declared nicotine a drug—finally—in 1995?

could use, "Kids need parents to instill in them that they can be comfortable within themselves. I think that's why kids start smoking." The teen correctly linked emotional distress about identity with cigarette smoking.

The viewpoints of a number of teens interviewed may be helpful to parents. Teens talking to teens can be a powerful means of getting the "stop smoking" message across. Here's what they had to say.

"Many kids are rebellious and won't listen to their parents," one fifteen-year-old girl said. "They feel their parents don't understand them. Sometimes their parents aren't there for them. Too often, kids are left unattended. And there's a lot of smoking, drinking, or using drugs in some kids' backgrounds. Parents need to be patient with their teenagers. They need to talk to them. My parents taught me that I can always change. They taught me to try, to give my best. They always told me I could do it. They told me if I got an F in school, I could turn it into an A if I worked hard enough. When I was ten, my parents gave me a journal so I could write my honest feelings. They trust me and they have never read my journal. Writing in my journal has helped me reflect and see my life differently. My parents taught me to be a leader, not a follower. I thought about smoking and what it would do to me. I have never smoked. I know how it would affect me."

WHEN TEENS TRY TO QUIT

The positive influence of the parents on this teenage girl is unmistakable. She was encouraged to think for herself, to keep a journal of her thoughts and feelings, and to learn to listen to her parents and trust what they had to say. She provides a powerful example that can be followed to help prevent a teen from starting to smoke, and that can be used to help a teen who wants to kick the habit.

A high school junior, who began smoking at age eleven or twelve, described his attempts to stop smoking. "My first attempt failed," he said. "But I tried to quit again. In fact, I've tried four or five times. I tried to cut back gradually, but that didn't work. I tried not smoking when I'm at school as a start, but that didn't work. I know that no good comes from smoking. My friends are on my back to quit. I used to think it relieved tension, but now I know that it doesn't. I've tried to quit cold turkey, but I haven't been able to stop." He spoke about how he was starting to really feel, for the first time, that he was addicted to cigarettes. However, the young man then asserted, "But I could quit after this pack!" He told how disappointed he felt in himself for not being able to quit. "I really felt bad when I smoked while I was baby-sitting recently." He knew about the dangers of second-hand smoke. "But I quit again recently. I'm dating a girl who has mood swings whenever I smoke. She says I smell of smoke all over, all the time. And she can't stand it. I'm quitting for her."

This teen said that his classmates—those who smoked and those who didn't—all told him that he couldn't quit smoking for his girlfriend. Everyone told him he had to quit for himself. But he didn't quite believe them. One girl told him, "If you quit for her, you'll be smoking again the minute you break up!"

It is difficult for teenagers to break a habit that began when many were children. Imagine—a fifteen-year-old who began smoking at age eleven has been a smoker for nearly 25 percent of his life! That is a crime that Big Tobacco has never had to pay for. Both of this young man's parents were heavy smokers during his childhood. However, he said that his father had successfully quit, cold turkey. "My mom quit, but she's started smoking again."

A girl in her sophomore year explained, "I smoked sometimes at parties. When everyone smoked, I smoked. Sometimes I smoked with friends. I smoked to feel relaxed. But I don't smoke now. I saw a video about smoking in which a woman became extremely ill and died." The young woman said she was greatly affected by the video, but she also didn't like how smoking made everything smell bad, how it changed the taste of foods. "I did a lot of smoking research and even did a science project about smoking in the sixth grade. I got a plastic bottle and a straw and a cigarette. The bottle was the lungs; the straw was the throat. I put a lit cigarette in the straw and we saw what happened to the lungs from the smoke. Everything turned black and got destroyed. Kids smoke for may reasons. To rebel, to get back at their parents, because they think it makes them feel relaxed. It doesn't. I think a lot of kids smoke because there is trouble in the home. Family life is the key. It's important how your parents treat you. My stepfather was given a cigarette by his father when he was only ten years old."

The young woman's story illustrates many of the themes of this book: the importance of the home environment, the role of peer pressure, and the positive impact education and information can have on a teenager.

Another teenage girl interviewed for this book said, "My mom quit smoking when I was ten years old. She became pregnant then. My mother is a big influence on me today. She is a really important role model for me. I don't smoke and never have because I saw a lot of people in my family die because of cigarette smoking. I never knew my grandfather because he smoked and died of cancer. I think they all died from lung cancer. My aunt and uncle still smoke, but my parents don't. There is a lot of pressure for teens to smoke. There are ads everywhere. I think they are more important than peer pressure. There is more of an effort to get teens hooked. It's all about the money that's involved for business."

A fifteen-year-old sophomore, who began smoking when he was ten, told what made him quit. "I had just started the tenth grade when I saw my little brother smoking. I told him to put that cigarette out, that it was wrong for him to be smoking. He said, 'You do it! Why can't I?' My little brother had a point. And I didn't have an answer. If I smoke, why can't he? I decided that I had to quit smoking. I told my little brother that having fun is better than smoking. I did a lot of things with him. I showed him more creative things to do than smoke. We began to exercise together, play baseball, run track. When we stopped smoking, we got closer. After I quit, I began to feel better. I had more energy. My stamina improved. I didn't tire as easily. I felt more motivated." This young man became involved in performing as a stand-up comedian and is considering studying acting. He works with a group that brings the anti-smoking message into junior high schools. The high school students perform skits with smoking-related themes and then the older students speak with the younger ones after the performance.

In addition, this young man is now trying to influence his mother, to help her quit smoking. "My mother still smokes. I even tried to get her to quit when I was still smoking. She says she's going to stop. I tell her, 'You're my mom! I care for you!' She recently got bronchitis and cut down on smoking. But she still smokes."

A high school teenager, who never smoked, also described trying to influence his mother to quit smoking. "I was always nagging my mother to stop smoking. Once I even threw her cigarettes away, but that didn't work. I asked her to quit as a birthday present for me. So far, she has been away from cigarettes for one year. But she still keeps them in the house. My mother's mother, father, sister, and brother all smoke. My mother's grandfather smoked and got cancer. He had a laryngectomy and later died from a heart attack." Despite the family history of smoking, this young man has not ever smoked a cigarette. "I didn't smoke because I wanted to play sports. I didn't want smoking to interfere with what I really wanted to do. I was on the swimming team and I play on my high school soccer team and on two other soccer teams. I want to excel at what I do and I want to enjoy life. Smoking has no part in that way of life."

Because this young man wanted to excel at sports, he did not smoke. His positive interests outweighed the lure of cigarettes. If a parent can enlist a teen's positive energy to accomplish a desired goal, cigarettes may quickly go by the board. When smoking interferes with something the teen loves, it is much easier to kick the habit.

One sixteen-year-old girl, a high school junior, actually quit smoking the day she was being interviewed for this book. She was challenged to do so by her peers because of a certain claim she made. "I started smoking when I was about ten. But I don't smoke that much." When asked how much she smoked, she was evasive. "I don't know, but not a lot. But I have been smoking all the time since I was ten. My mother used to ask me to light her cigarettes for her when I was little. I liked to do it. I also used to go to the store when I was a kid and buy cigarettes for my mother. Then I started to buy them for myself. They sold them to me. It was no problem. They also sell loose cigarettes to kids. I smoke and I enjoy it but I can quit any time I want to. I just don't want to, that's all. I could quit right now if I wanted to," she said proudly.

The other teens present laughed at her claim. Some of her peers were smokers; others had recently quit; still others had never smoked. But all challenged her to quit right there, on the spot. Backed into a corner, unwilling to take back her boast, she announced she was stopping smoking. On a follow-up interview, about a month later, she had not returned to smoking. "I

feel great," she said. "I have more energy. I'm playing hand-
ball, basketball, and softball. And I'm really enjoying it. I have
a lot more stamina than when I was smoking. My family has
noticed I've quit. My older sister is so proud of me. And all my
friends notice that I've quit. I don't want to smoke anymore.
There's no peer pressure to smoke. Even my friends who smoke
say 'More power to you!' And I have more money in my pocket.
I never knew how much money I was spending on cigarettes.
Now I can spend that money on other things."

THE BENEFITS OF QUITTING

As these stories illustrate, it is difficult to quit smoking but it
is possible and the rewards are great. Teens who make it through
to the other side find that they have increased energy, are more
active, enjoy life more, and have a lot more money in their pockets that they can spend on things that really interest them.

The beneficial effects of quitting smoking start within minutes and last for a lifetime. Within twenty minutes of stopping
smoking, blood pressure and heart rate return to normal. The
teen will begin to feel calmer and more relaxed. It will be obvious that cigarettes make one more tense, not more relaxed.
Within three hours, the carbon monoxide level in the blood—
which is at a high level in smokers—returns to normal. In the
same time period, the oxygen level in the blood returns to normal. This results in a feeling of increased energy and vitality.
Within twenty-four hours, the increased risk of a heart attack

later in life begins to decrease. Within forty-eight hours, the sense of taste and smell return to normal. Within three weeks, circulation improves and lung function increases by at least 30 percent. Within one to nine months, the smoker's cough, sinus congestion, fatigue, and shortness of breath all decrease. The body's overall energy level increases dramatically. Within only one year, the risk of coronary heart disease is cut in half.

And the benefits derived from stopping smoking continue to grow, day by day, year after year.

Teens need to know that they can stop smoking and that their parents are there to help them do it. They also need to know that it may not be easy. It takes the average person who quits smoking about four or five tries before succeeding. In addition, each teen needs to find the smoking cessation techniques that works best for him or her. For some, cold turkey is the only way to go. Others may respond better to an organized smoking cessation program, of which there are many. Still other teens may want to use one of the various smoking cessation products that are now on the market, such as the nicotine patch, nicotine spray, or nicotine gum.

But whatever method works, it is important that teenagers realize that quitting smoking is probably the single most important thing they can do to improve their health and increase their enjoyment of life.

CHAPTER THREE
What the Experts Say

"SMOKING ACTUALLY FULFILLS A VARIETY OF FUNCTIONS IN THE EVERYDAY LIVES OF MANY ADOLESCENTS."
—FROM *SMOKING IN ADOLESCENCE*
BY BARBARA LLOYD AND KEVIN LUCAS

There are experts who use well-designed studies to investigate the phenomenon of teenage smoking. There are also experts who work with teenagers on a daily basis, frequently in a school setting. Although they have widely divergent methods, and often come to greatly differing conclusions, each contributes important information that can help parents who are trying to help their teenagers stop smoking.

WORKING WITH TEENS WHO SMOKE

One counselor interviewed for this book, a professional with about five years experience in the field, worked in a public school for gifted children in a major metropolitan area. The school has an excellent reputation and is even known nationally. Its graduates attend the finest colleges and universities in the United States. The student body is comprised of extremely bright teenage boys and girls of all races, religions, and ethnic backgrounds. In a sense, they are among the nation's best and brightest. "I'd estimate that about 30 to 40 percent of our students smoke," the counselor said. "In our school, we have four counselors for 2,600 students."

During a visit to the school, the counselor asked a student if he would be interviewed for this book under conditions of complete confidentiality. A bright student, he could not stop smoking and was beginning to cut class because he needed to get his nicotine fix. His grades were suffering. Yet, he believed smoking helped him concentrate and improve his academic performance. The young man said smoking had not begun to affect his health, yet he explained that his athletic performance was suffering because smoking was reducing his stamina. After a brief interview, the student made an appointment to see the counselor at the end of the day and returned to class. What can counselors in a school setting realistically hope to achieve in terms of reducing or preventing teen smoking when there is only one counselor for every 700 or 800 students?

"I have a slightly different approach," the counselor said. "I try to show students that our bodies are temples and that caring for their bodies is a gift they can give to life. My approach includes a kind of generic spirituality that even agnostics or atheists can accept."

Another counselor at a public school, a young man relatively new to the field, was interviewed for this book. In his opinion, teens talking to other teens about smoking can often produce excellent results. "I think a desire to belong plays a big role in kids starting smoking. A lot of kids today lack a family connection. And sometimes tobacco use brings peer acceptance. Tobacco advertising can be a big enticement to teenagers. They show beautiful women and real men. The ads portray images of success and having it all. In our school, we have a program—Teens Against Teens Using—or TATU. In this program, we use a wide variety of methods to help keep kids tobacco-free. For example, we show kids tobacco ads and have them express what they think about it. Peer education is the underlying principle of TATU."

During a visit to the school, a group of teenagers engaged in a vigorous discussion of tobacco advertising. Many of the teens saw clearly how the ads attempted to exploit them. However, some of the teens who understood how Big Tobacco was using them were smokers nonetheless. A few of them understood why and could admit it: they were addicted. "A lot of this is beyond our control," the young counselor acknowledged. "We can show support and encouragement but we are limited by many factors." To reduce teen smoking, he felt, parents need to be involved.

Another counselor, with over twenty years of experience working with teenagers, said, "It is almost a teenager's job to take risks. It's their job to find out who they are. Some look at teenage involvement in risky behavior as rebellion. But that's negative. A positive way of looking at the situation is to see that teens are exploring. They are involved in personality testing; they are seeking identities." In her experience, counselors who focus on the positive aspect of teen behavior—even risky behavior—have a chance of making some headway with adolescents. "We put information out there for teenagers—about smoking, about drinking alcohol or using drugs, about pregnancy, STDs or AIDS—so that teenagers can make their own decisions. It's a dilemma," she said.

Teens need to learn to make their own decision. To do so, they need information. But how much information is enough, how much is too much? It is difficult for many parents to trust that their teens will make the right decisions. "Many parents have low expectations of their kids," the counselor said. "My experience shows that parents should not underestimate their teenagers."

For the professionals who work in the schools counseling teenagers, smoking is a serious problem but it is just one of many. Teen suicide, depression and anxiety, physical and sexual abuse, alcohol and drug abuse, serious emotional disorders, and violence all are part of the daily lives of too many teens today. "We show our concern," one counselor said. "We don't have the perfect answer. In my work, I do what I can to help kids feel better about themselves. A kid with a positive self-image is less likely to smoke. Teenage depression is regularly undiagnosed and untreated. I think that smoking often masks depression. I think that we must deal with teenage depression if we want to do something about teen smoking."

In addition to learning from their hands-on work with teenagers, counselors also benefit from the work and insights of those in academia who study teenage behavior at somewhat of a distance. The information that is compiled from studies of adolescent smoking in nations all over the world can be helpful to parents as well as professionals.

RESEARCH ON TEEN SMOKING

A wide range of research has produced a significant body of evidence about many aspects of teenage smoking. However, a good number of adult moral value judgments have made their way into the "objective" scientific research reports. Adoles-

cent smoking is too often viewed only from an adult perspective. Researchers describe "risk behaviors" such as cigarette
smoking, alcohol and drug abuse or thrill-seeking, and link
them with adolescent sexual activity in what they call a "syndrome of problem behaviors." Is it really helpful—or even accurate—to consider a destructive activity such as cigarette
smoking as the equivalent of a natural biological activity such
as sexual expression?

The so-called risk behaviors—activities that present an
immediate or long-range threat to health—are a part of everyday adult life. Teens see this clearly and often reject what they
see as hypocritical adult advice, namely "Do as I say, not as I
do." Today, a number of researchers are attempting to replace
adult moral judgments of adolescent smoking with an understanding of the meaning of smoking to teens themselves.

The "theory of problem behaviors" that was first promoted
over twenty years ago may be a problem in itself. In the 1960s,
in the United States, Great Britain, and Europe, a "youth culture" developed that challenged adult authority and changed
society dramatically within one generation. A great deal of
social research was done to understand the origins of the revolutionary changes young people were initiating. Core beliefs
about society, the family, sexual life, education, the workplace,
and religious faith were reevaluated. Attitudes toward drinking alcohol, smoking cigarettes, and using drugs were changing as well. *Many of the adults now reading this book were those
young people.*

Two researchers, Richard and Shirley Jessor, had a profound impact on research about teenagers in America. They are the founders of the "problem behavior theory." They devised a three-part system to understand teenage behavior which consisted of the *personality system,* the *perceived environment system,* and the *behavior system.* The researchers studied how teens develop goals in life and what social factors influence that development; what external factors restrain teen behavior; and what inner mechanisms inhibit "unconventional" teen behavior. In addition, they studied the way teens perceive their environment—parents, family, school, friends, peers—and how that perception shapes teenage behavior. It was found that teens who had a greater identification with their parents were more conventional in their behavior; teens who identified more with their peers tended to be more experimental in their behavior. Based on their research, Jessor and Jessor defined what they called a syndrome of problem behavior.

The theory of problem behavior was shaped as part of an effort to understand the challenge the youth of the 1960s and early 1970s presented to authority. Since then, values have changed dramatically. Over the past twenty-five years, the list of problem behaviors has continued to grow and many researchers are now questioning this point of view. For example, the concept of "sensation-seeking" is now considered by many experts to be a more realistic explanation of teen smoking than the theory of problem behaviors.

This influential theory has been the subject of hundreds of published studies recently and involves a complex, multifaceted analysis of psychological, physiological, and genetic factors. One researcher has developed a sensation-seeking scale (SSS) that can be used to predict the likelihood of such teen behavior as smoking. Four main factors are involved:

Thrill and adventure seeking: risky physical activity; certain organized sports with an element of danger; moderately frightening experiences.

Experience seeking: a bohemian, "Beat," hippie or other nonconformity; interest in traveling, music and art, writing.

Disinhibition: attraction to unconventional behavior, even the illegal kind.

Boredom susceptibility: a low tolerance to routine; increased sensation seeking.

Teens who score high on the SSS rating scale were much more likely to become smokers than were teens with low scores. These results held true over a ten-year period of testing. The sensation-seeking theory also held true for teens from a wide range of cultural backgrounds. Studies of adolescents in the United States, the United Kingdom, Norway, the Netherlands, and Israel all showed comparable results.

Teens with high SSS scores were also more likely to use and abuse alcohol, smoke marijuana, and take such drugs as cocaine, barbiturates, amphetamines, and opiates. In addition, high-risk sexual behavior was more likely with these teens. The

SSS results echoed the findings of the earlier studies based on the theory of problem behavior. Some researchers have found that cigarette smoking alone is an indicator that a teen may engage in high-risk sexual activity. However, not all experts agree with the sensation-seeking explanation and not all studies support this view.

PROTECTIONS AGAINST TEEN SMOKING

Recent research suggests that there is a relationship between risk factors and protective factors that has been long overlooked. Among the protective factors researchers have uncovered are a positive outlook toward school; a positive orientation toward health; good relations with adults; strong ties to generally accepted societal values; strong religious feelings; a sense of and acceptance of parental and societal limits; friends who are well-adapted to society; and involvement in positive social activities, such as volunteer work. Among the risk factors for teen smoking are a negative orientation toward school; doubt that life will be happy and successful; low self-esteem; friends who smoke or engage in other risky behaviors; a feeling of hopelessness; and stronger ties to friends than to parents.

There is a connection between a teenager's perception of his or her parenting and later substance abuse, such as smoking. Parental support may be present but the teen may not feel it is there. A number of studies suggest that the lack of a strong bond between parents and children increases the likelihood of teen smoking. Parental support and control, parental affection, support from other adults, and community involvement all play key roles in an adolescent's life. The presence or absence of these factors helps determine whether or not a teenager begins smoking.

The experts have found that these protective factors do not entirely eliminate the possibility of a teen smoking. But they do minimize the risk. And these positive factors were found to be of value in studies of teens of both genders from all ethnic and racial backgrounds. The risk factors seemed to make teens more vulnerable to peer pressure and to violating social codes and mores. Researchers also found that adolescents from lower socioeconomic groups who have low self-esteem were even more vulnerable to the lure of cigarette smoking. In fact, the *New York Times* reported recently that smoking among pregnant teenagers has increased, especially among Mexican-American, Puerto Rican, and black teens. Recent reports that overall smoking among black teenagers—a group whose rates of smoking are lower than any other group of teens—is on the rise.

When it comes to teen smoking, the relationship between risk factors and protective factors is complex. In one study, teens and adults were asked to rate the consequences of engaging in such activities as smoking, drinking, and taking drugs. Researchers found that the adult and teen responses were similar. However, the experts found that although most smokers agreed that smoking was injurious to their health, their most basic beliefs about smoking were not related to health at all. Many smokers know the physical risks of smoking, and know they can avoid those risks by quitting, but they smoke for other reasons that just quitting smoking does not help them with. Quitting alone does not provide anything to take the place smoking plays in their lives.

ADULT THINKING VS. TEEN THINKING

Adult perceptions of risk and adolescent perceptions of risk are not always the same. Adults and teens make decisions in quite different ways. Adolescents do not yet have the experience or the skills to make certain decisions. To gain the necessary knowledge to make mature decisions, teens must first make mistakes. In fact, the whole period of life between childhood and adulthood is one of learning by trial and error. This view was promoted by the influential psychologist Erik Erickson. Unfortunately, starting smoking may be one of these mistakes; nicotine addiction compounds the problem.

One study comparing adult and adolescent decision-making uncovered a number of factors that were involved in determining whether a course of action (or inaction) was risky and then deciding whether or not to take that risk: identifying the choices one had; estimating the consequences of the action or inaction; evaluating the likely consequences of each possibility; assessing the likelihood of each outcome; and combining all four factors and making a decision.

The researchers found that adult and teen decision-making was different in every stage of the decision-making process. In general, adults saw more courses of actions than teens did. And adults were better able to think through the consequences of taking—or not taking—an action. Adult and teen values were different as well. For example, teens valued peer approval more than adults did. And teens found such activities as hunting and mountain climbing less risky than adults did.

Teen perceptions of risks and of risky behavior, and teen values, were often based on a lack of life experience. In contrast, adults perceptions and values were shaped by their life experiences. A substantial body of research suggests that adolescence is a time during which teens develop a sense of "personal meaning." Teens gradually learn who they are and come to better understand themselves, their parents, and their peers. They become more able to judge what is risky and what the outcome of specific choices may be. The more a teen is able to incorporate this information into her life, the better decisions she will make.

All of this learning takes place in a psychological and social environment that is always changing for the teenager. It is apparent that the meaning of smoking to the teenager must be understood if teen smoking is to be prevented and eliminated.

STUDIES OF TEEN SMOKING

It is difficult to study teen smoking because the situation can change rapidly for each teen. For example, a teen who reports that he has smoked a few cigarettes within the past week may quit the next week. However, he would be counted as a smoker. And a teen who says she is an occasional smoker today, may be a regular smoker in a short period of time and not be counted correctly in the results. One study of New Zealand teens found that regular teen smokers and nonsmokers accurately identified themselves 95 percent of the time. However, nearly half of the teens who were occasional smokers were incorrectly identified as nonsmokers.

Researchers have found that a single questionnaire is not enough to gather accurate, usable information about teen smoking. A number of surveys must be conducted over a period of time to gather the quality of information needed to reach valid conclusions about adolescent smoking.

One aspect of teen smoking that is too often overlooked is *pleasure*. Many researchers report that teenagers find smoking to be a pleasurable activity. This sensation of pleasure is separate from the "rush" of nicotine or the reduction in stress that many adolescents achieve when smoking. Teens enjoy the look, the feel, and the design elements of their particular brand of cigarette. They enjoy lighting up, taking that first puff, blowing smoke rings. For many teens, smoking is also a way to pass the time when bored or restless.

Teenagers also frequently use smoking as a "social lubricant." Cigarettes can play a role in establishing friendships, breaking the ice with members of the opposite sex, and becoming a member of a desired group. In this way, smoking helps a teen establish an identity. A number of studies conducted in many different countries have looked at teen images of smokers and nonsmokers. Teens who smoke, or who say they intend to smoke, have highly favorable images of smokers. This influences them to want to belong to groups of teens who are smokers.

Investigators have found that the first smoking experience was either an experiment, motivated out of curiosity, or else resulted from peer pressure. Contrary to popular belief, the first smoking experience was not always described as an unpleasant event by teens. In general, it took time for smoking to "hook" the teens studied. It also took time for the teenagers to get used to smoking, at which point they said they liked smoking. A number of girls admitted that one day they realized that smoking had changed for them—*they had become addicted.*

The evidence seems to indicate clearly that teenage girls smoke more than teenage boys and that this pattern has remained constant for years. One study found that at age twelve, boys and girls smoked the same number of cigarettes, but that in later years, girls smoked more than boys. It seems that simply being a girl puts a teen at a higher risk of becoming a regular smoker. A number of theories—psychoanalytical, social learning, and cognitive-developmental—have been put forward by experts to explain this finding.

Body image may play a role here. It seems that girls are more concerned with body image than boys. Many studies suggest that girls as young as five years old, inundated by distorted mass media images of women, are already concerned about their looks and their weight. There is some evidence to indicate that girls may smoke to help control their weight. Also, many teens believe that cigarette smoking helps to reduce stress.

Teenage girls consistently report higher levels of stress in their lives than do teenage boys. A number of studies indicate that teenage girls are particularly vulnerable to stress and may turn to smoking as a means of coping with this stress.

However, it is not clear that anyone has yet come up with the definitive answer as to why girls smoke more than boys.

Class is a phenomenon usually more associated with Britain than the United States (which imagines itself to be a classless society). However, there does seem to be a link between social class and teen smoking. Investigators in the United States, Scotland, and Canada have all reported such a link. One British researcher reported that workingclass girls in English secondary schools were more likely to smoke than were girls from higher social echelons. A study of Dutch teens found that workingclass adolescents were more likely to describe smoking as pleasurable, while middle-class teens were more likely to be nonsmokers, citing health risks as reasons for not smoking. These studies suggest that smoking is an integral part of workingclass life.

However, not all experts have come up with the same results. One study of English teens found that there seemed to be no relationship between social class and teen smoking. Another study of younger teens in Scotland also concluded that there was no direct link between social status and teen cigarette smoking. The same Scottish researchers did find a link between class and smoking in older teens, as did an American study of older teenagers.

Although there is disagreement among the experts on the role social class plays in teen smoking, there is a general consensus that parental smoking and parental educational levels have a great influence on the smoking behavior of teenagers.

Black teenagers have been reported to smoke less than white teenagers in North America in a large number of studies conducted over many years. This is a consistent pattern, although the most recent evidence suggests that more black teenagers in the United States are taking up smoking. Native American teens appear to smoke more than white or Hispanic teenagers.

These differing rates of teen smoking may be due to varying patterns of parental and peer smoking among the different ethnic groups. In all ethnic groups, teens who had close peers and siblings who smoked were more likely to smoke themselves. White teenagers were more likely to smoke if a parent smoked, but this was not true for black teens. One study reported that parental smoking, peer-group smoking, parent educational level, and teen educational level did not have an impact on smoking by black adolescents.

Another U.S. study found that white teenagers who had a best friend who smoked were twice as likely to smoke as teens whose best friends did not smoke. This was not true, however, for black teenagers. Having a best friend who smoked had no impact at all. For Hispanic-American adolescents, some studies suggest that the more these teens adapt American values, the more likely they are to smoke. Other studies of adolescents who have migrated to America indicate that the stress of the change in their lives contributes to higher rates of smoking.

Educational level seems to affect rates of smoking as well. Smoking is more prevalent among teens with parents who have lower educational levels than among teens whose parents have greater academic achievement. Increased educational levels in the U.S., some studies suggest, have contributed to lower rates of smoking. For example, between 1974 and 1985, smoking among college students dropped by 10 percent; smoking fell among those with some college by 8.6 percent; smoking decreased among high school graduates by only 3.3 percent; and smoking declined by only 2.1 percent among high school dropouts.

It seems that teenagers who have a high degree of commitment to doing well in school, and to obtaining a high level of academic achievement, are less likely to become smokers than teens who do not value their education as much. This finding did not apply only to American teenagers. One group of investigators looked at smoking and educational attitudes in eleven European nations and found that there was a link between smoking and negative attitudes toward school. There were links between smoking and poor academic performance, as well as between smoking and aspirations toward higher academic levels. The researchers felt that a supportive school environment could offer teens protection from cigarette smoking.

Other investigators have suggested that teen smoking may be an ineffective way of rebelling, asserting independence, or finding acceptance among peers. There is evidence to indicate that, among such teenagers, the need for adult approval is less important than for nonsmoking teens. To such adolescents, smoking is a way of appearing adult themselves. A recent study of American high school seniors suggests that this may be true.

Sports seem to play a protective role for teenagers in terms of smoking. Girls who are involved in organized sports are much less likely to smoke. However, girls who are involved in organized social activities are more likely to smoke. Researchers have discovered that teenage boys who did not intend to smoke were more physically fit, participated more frequently in organized sports, watched less TV, and were less likely to drink alcohol than teenage boys who said they intended to smoke.

Researchers in Iceland found that Icelandic teenagers who took part in team sports were less likely to smoke or drink alcohol than other teens. However, they found that teens who were involved with individual sports activities did not show such a benefit. In Finland, investigators found that teens who did not participate in sports had higher rates of smoking cigarettes and drinking alcohol than teens who participated in sports. This held true for both boys and girls. American researchers who have studied high school students have found results similar to those in Finland.

SMOKING AND THE FAMILY

One expert looked at the symbolic aspect of smoking for teenagers—a means of challenging adult authority and expressing individuality and autonomy. According to this expert's view, teens who participate in organized sports are taking part in officially approved activities and making their way to adulthood and maturity in a conventional manner. Teens who smoke, on the other hand, are rebelling and making the transition to adult life in an unconventional manner, in defiance of the adult world.

The home environment may be the key to adolescent smoking. The nuclear families of *Father Knows Best, Leave It to Beaver,* and *Ozzie and Harriet* may live on courtesy of cable TV, but over the past thirty years, the traditional family structure has undergone profound changes. Many studies have shown the strong impact family life has on teen smoking. Some medically oriented studies postulate an "epidemic" model for the transmission of smoking from parents or older siblings to teens. Some investigations of American adolescents indicate that teens whose parents smoke progress rapidly from experimenting with cigarette smoking to becoming regular smokers. A recent English study produced similar findings.

In terms that are not accepted by all researchers, investigators talk of "inheriting smoking"; of smoking as a "social contagion"; or of "intergenerational transmission" of smoking. One Dutch study claimed that 59 percent of smoking behavior could be caused by environmental factors and 31 percent to genetic factors. Not all in the field accept these medical models of smoking. Some researchers do not even accept that there is a direct link between parental smoking and teen smoking. In fact, one extensive study of American teens found that parental smoking had very little effect on teen smoking. Peer influence was found to be far greater than parental influence. An Australian study concluded that peers who smoked had far more influence on teen smoking than parents who smoked. Another Australian study found that teens' role models are their peers; by contrast, parents represent standards of "normal," accepted behavior. Two American studies—one of high school students, the other of seventh-graders—support the findings of the Australian researchers. A number of experts have found evidence that peer influence increases with age during the teen years. One study showed that, among eleven-year-olds, parents were more influential than peers, but that by the age of fourteen, peers exerted more influence than parents.

Many researchers are now studying family function and dysfunction in an attempt to understand teen smoking. Many of these experts believe that teen smoking is inextricably linked with family functioning and the quality of relationships within the family.

The United States has the highest divorce rate in the world. In the United Kingdom, during the decade of the 1990s, about 100,000 couples with children under the age of sixteen were divorced each year. As traumatic as divorce is to children, the conditions at home that led up to the divorce can be equally as difficult. Current research shows that there is evidence of problems among children of divorce long before the divorce actually occurs. Rather, it may be the tension in the home in the years leading up to divorce—rather than divorce itself—that may be responsible for such behaviors as teen smoking. Many researchers insist that quality of home life and teen smoking are inseparable.

A significant number of studies have found that teen smoking rates are higher in what some now call "non-standard families." Researchers have found patterns of increased smoking among teens raised in family structures other than the traditional nuclear family model in the United States and the United Kingdom. In one large study conducted in Finland, it was found that teens raised in "non-standard" families were much more likely to smoke than adolescents raised by both biological parents. Scottish researchers found similar results. One group of American investigators found a link, not only between parental smoking and teen smoking, but also between teen smoking and family disharmony. Another American research study demonstrated that family troubles and poor family functioning can be predictive of later teen smoking. The latest research suggests that poor family functioning influences teen smoking independently of parental smoking.

TWO BRITISH STUDIES

The British government, like its American counterpart, is extremely concerned about the consequences of teen smoking, especially among girls between the ages of thirteen to fifteen. Two studies by British researchers investigated aspects of the problem: one looked at the high rate of smoking among teenage girls in Britain; the other investigated factors that may help prevent and reduce teen smoking.

The study of teenage girls looked at such factors as age, gender, attitudes about smoking, social environment, body image, stress, and social identity. The researchers investigated how each of these factors related to smoking. A second study looked at the meaning of smoking for teens. These researchers have come up with new concepts about what is involved in getting teens to stop smoking. In the second study, researchers looked at the links between smoking and social class, gender, peer groups, school environment, family life, teen images and identities, and health beliefs.

The two investigations—called the Sussex study and the London study—used different methodologies but reported consistent results. The investigators focused on two questions. First, why do young teenage girls smoke? Second, how can young teenagers be protected from smoking?

The Sussex study looked at factors that influenced young girls to smoke. The London study was conducted in a manner that allowed participating teens to learn from each phase of the investigation and to come to understand more about their smoking behavior. Both studies sought to uncover patterns in teenage smoking.

The London study looked at the teens' smoking; family smoking; smoking-related attitudes and experiences; health beliefs and state of health; community activities and peer relationships. The researchers were looking for ways to prevent teens from starting to smoke and ways to help them stop smoking. The Sussex study focused on teenage girls' social identities and their images of smokers and nonsmokers. To establish "social identities," the teens were asked to use certain descriptive terms. Nonsmokers were frequently describe as uncool, wimpish, dull, doesn't like to party, doesn't like the opposite sex. Smokers were frequently described as cool, tough, exciting, likes partying, attractive to the opposite sex.

The Sussex results showed that smoking increased among all levels of British students over the school year. For example, in Year 7, only 0.6 percent of the teens were smokers at the start of the school year, whereas 3.4 percent were regular smokers by the end of the school year. In Year 8, the percentage of regular smokers increased from 4.3 percent to 12.2 percent; in Year 9 from 9.4 percent to 16.9 percent; in Year 10 from 19.1 percent to 28.0 percent; and in Year 11 from 26.9 percent to 32.8 percent. The increase in regular smoking involved both boys and girls.

The investigators found that the proportion of occasional smokers remained constant throughout the study and they considered this highly significant. According to the researchers occasional smoking is a transitional phase. A teen who is an occasional smoker may become a regular smoker or may stop smoking completely. The London study results showed that 12 percent of regular smokers were aged thirteen or under; 15 percent were age fourteen; and 73 percent were ages fifteen to sixteen.

Regular smokers were more likely to drink alcohol and smoke marijuana. In the United Kingdom, unlike in the United States, marijuana is regularly smoked mixed with tobacco. Some researchers suggest that some teens may be introduced to tobacco through marijuana, and not vice versa.

These two studies produced interesting findings concerning parenting styles and teen smoking. Authoritarian parenting methods were found to be linked with teen smoking, as were stern discipline and poor communication. These findings were true across all socioeconomic groups. The findings of the London study indicate that family structure and functioning clearly influence teen smoking. The quality of the relationship between parent and teen is critical. Both parents and teens emphasized the importance of mutual respect and open communication. And both parents and teens said that trust was essential—if not the key—to a positive relationship. Adolescents and parents recognized that where there was open communication, mutual respect, and trust, there was less likelihood of a teen starting to smoke cigarettes. It is also only in such an atmosphere that a teenager who smokes will feel able to reach out and ask for help.

The researchers in the London study found that authoritarian parental behavior fostered lack of respect, secrecy, and mistrust. Teens only trusted parents who respected and trusted them. The results of the study also revealed that adolescent and parental perceptions differed significantly on key points. Parents were more likely to believe that the lines of communication were open and that communication was good. Teens disagreed. Teens frequently said that *their* views were never included in the discussions with their parents. About 40 percent of teens thought that talking about "risky behaviors" would *never* affect their behavior; only 10 percent of parents felt this way. About 60 percent of parents believed that talking about smoking could often change a teenager's behavior; only about 20 percent of teens felt this way.

In the Sussex study, researchers found that about 50 percent of teens who had parents who smoked tried cigarettes themselves. And two out of three teens who had an older sibling who smoked tried smoking for themselves. In families where parents or siblings were smoking currently, teens had a two-fold risk of smoking cigarettes themselves compared to teens in families where there was no smoking. In homes where parents and older siblings smoked, teens were at a four-fold risk of starting smoking. Perhaps most important, the research shows that teenagers themselves feel that their own parents' smoking contributed to their starting smoking. In families where parents and siblings never smoked, it was highly unlikely for teens to begin smoking.

The essence of adolescence itself is change. And today's teens live in a world that is changing as rapidly as their own bodies. Increasingly, both parents are not present to raise the children. If they are, both parents may work outside the home. Children are either raised by strangers or left to fend for themselves as "latch-key" kids. As a result, schools have come to bear many of the responsibilities for children that were formerly the duties of parents. And television has become a dominant force in the lives of teenagers. Many teens spend more time each week watching television than they do in school. Teens are lucky if they get thirty minutes a day to talk to their parents.

One researcher investigated this complex and frustrating state of affairs—for both parents and children—and summarized his findings. The evidence suggested that there were four major factors involved in parenting that were essential in helping children develop in ways that enabled them to interact with their peers and environment successfully:

Parental affection—this helps shape children's involvement with one another.

Parental discipline—too much or too little results in problems for children.

Parental involvement—gives children a sense of security.

Family democracy—helps children develop the skills needed to work well with others.

The experts say that most adolescents appear better able to stand up for themselves and to interact well with their peers when the above conditions are present in family life. Preparing youngsters to function well with their peers is critical in terms of smoking because peer groups play such an important role in encouraging or discouraging a teen to smoke. Adolescents understand what peer pressure is and how it works. Invariably, however, teens believe that peer pressure affects other teens, not themselves. An individual teenager is not likely to accept that he or she is smoking as a result of peer pressure.

THE POWER OF PEERS

Recent studies of American adolescents have shown that ineffective parenting—too harsh or too lax—contributed significantly to teens associating with "the wrong crowd." The investigators also found links between ineffective parenting and teen smoking, especially between the ages of thirteen and sixteen.

The experts say that the effects of peer groups on teen smoking are thoroughly documented. In one extremely large study of black and white American teenagers, ages twelve to seventeen, the researchers found that teen smoking was strongly associated with smoking by peers, especially by best friends. Researchers in Norway, New Zealand, Great Britain, and Jamaica have compiled results that confirm the findings of the American studies.

The experts have also found evidence that peer groups can help protect a teen. Friends can be a great influence not to smoke. This can be seen in team sports, for example. The team goals can be undermined if members of the team impair their athletic abilities by smoking. Team members can apply peer pressure to keep a teen from smoking. In the Sussex study, researchers discovered that only about 5 percent of teens who were nonsmokers had a best friend who smoked. Conversely, over 75 percent of regular smokers had a best friend who smoked.

The London study indicated that the nature of the teenagers' friendships and peer-group interactions played a critical role in teen smoking. Many researchers in North America, the United Kingdom, and Europe have found that teens regularly refer to what they call "real friends." The overwhelming majority of teens believe that a "real friend" who smokes would not attempt to persuade a good friend to smoke. And a "real friend" who did not smoke would try to influence a smoking friend to quit. All teens agreed, however, that friends should not pressure one another—they should simply be honest.

A number of studies suggest that groups of teens that smoke apply subtle, and not so subtle, pressure on nonsmoking teens to get them to pick up the habit. Investigators have identified three major forms of pressure: persuasion, physical intimidation, and ostracism. Although teens believe that friends should not encourage friends to start smoking, many do not behave that way, and groups of teenagers often try to get new friends to join them in smoking. Physical intimidation was not extremely common, but it was reported in some studies, such as the Sussex study, which involved teenage girls. Teenagers who did not begin to smoke when urged to do so by their smoking companions reported that they felt gradually isolated by the group. Some teens wanted to be a part of the group so much that they began to smoke; others found new friends.

Big Tobacco constantly presents cigarette smoking as a choice, not as an addiction. Its persistent repetition of this Big Lie has had an effect throughout society, with many people unwittingly echoing the propaganda of the tobacco industry. The research indicates that many teens view cigarette smoking as a matter of personal choice. Many teens report that, just as a "real friend" will not try to persuade a nonsmoker to start smoking, a "real" friend will respect another teen's decision to begin smoking cigarettes.

The good news in the current research on teen smoking is that, apparently, the longer a teenager resists cigarette smoking, the less likely he is to begin smoking at any time in the future. A young teen's ability to say no to peer pressure grows stronger with age and increasing maturity. However, research in this area also shows the importance of choosing friends wisely. There

DID YOU KNOW . . .

In 1896, the first matchbook tobacco ads appeared? About 100 years later, the first American Cancer Society matchless matchbooks appeared promoting a quit-smoking message.

In 1909, Honus Wagner, a Hall of Fame baseball player, demanded that his card be removed from circulation by a tobacco company that was distributing baseball cards?

In 1912, the first paper linking lung cancer and smoking was published.

In 1913, the first nationwide advertising campaign for a cigarette—Camels—began.

In 1947, the singer Tex Williams had a big hit with his song "Smoke! Smoke! Smoke!" In 1985, he died of lung cancer.

In 1955, acclaimed CBS newsman Edward R. Murrow produced a hard-hitting report on the hazards of cigarette smoking. Murrow, a chain smoker, died in 1965 of lung cancer.

Cigarettes contain acetylene, ammonia, benzene, cyanide, formaldehyde, and methanol.

It takes the average smoker five attempts at quitting before finally stopping smoking.

A person who smokes a pack a day loses seven years of life expectancy.

is evidence to indicate that a teen who is an occasional smoker (occasional smokers can go either way with smoking) and who has a best friend who smokes is twice as likely to become a regular smoker as a teen whose best friend is a nonsmoker.

In general, the experts conclude that, as adolescents move out of the sphere of influence of the family—a healthy and necessary development—and come to need and want the respect and friendship of peers, the influence of peers on smoking grows stronger. However, the experts emphasize that no one aspect of teen smoking can be understood in isolation. Parental smoking, smoking by family members, family structure and function, and the influence of peer groups all have profound impacts on teen smoking. And so does the school environment.

How Teens Use Cigarettes

Schools set different policies on teen smoking and on smoking by all adult employees of the school. Policies, guidelines, and rules have an important impact on the rates of teen smoking at individual schools. There is evidence to indicate that schools with more comprehensive no-smoking policies frequently graduate substantially fewer teens who smoke regularly than do schools that tolerate teen smoking, not literally on the school grounds but simply across the street.

The experts also stress the importance of smoking in relation to a teen's emotional life. Cigarettes are, basically, a drug-delivery system that brings a mood-enhancing chemical to the smoker. Adults use mood-enhancing drugs all the time: alcohol to celebrate, relax, or enhance a meal; caffeine for a morning or afternoon pick up; and thousands of over-the-counter drugs for a wide range of problems. Adolescents see this in the home, at school, at work, in the movies, and on television. Is it any surprise that teen behavior mirrors adult behavior?

According to the expert's evidence, teens use cigarettes for a wide variety of purposes: to help control stress or fight off the blues; to kill time and fight boredom; to help establish an identity among their peers; and for the pleasure involved in all the physical aspects of smoking.

Many adolescents report that smoking cigarettes helps them cope with the stress they feel in their lives, at home, at school, or with friends. Medical research indicates that stress is a significant cause of mental and physical health problems for teens. As with adults, teens feel stress from both major and minor life problems that pass, as well as from chronic life problems that persist for prolonged periods of time.

The research indicates that teenage girls perceive and report more intense feelings of stress than do boys. Some experts believe that this accounts for the higher rates of teen smoking among girls. Younger teenage girls appear to be the most vulnerable to the appeal of smoking. In addition, teenage girls have a higher incidence of depression and a number of researchers believe that depression is a factor that contributes to teenage smoking.

Experts in stress say that the difficulties adults and adolescents face come not from the stresses of life—they are usually unavoidable—but from the ineffective means people use to cope with stress. Cigarette smoking is a particularly harmful and ineffective way of attempting to manage the stresses of life. Teens may resort to smoking in response to stress from demanding external circumstances or in an attempt to control unwanted internal emotional states. Experts call these two forms of behavior problem-focused coping and emotion-focused coping.

Some studies indicate that girls may experience more stress than boys because they employ less-effective coping strategies. For example, girls are more likely to drift off into daydreaming and wishful thinking than are boys in response to stressful life circumstances. However, other investigations have shown, on the positive side, that girls are more likely to reach out for help than are boys. In addition, also on the positive side, girls are more likely to express their "negative" feelings—through crying or screaming—than are boys.

Other researchers have classified teen coping strategies as internal coping, active coping, and withdrawal. Internal coping involves introspection, thinking, and searching for a solution to a problem. Active coping involves reaching out to others for help with a problem. Withdrawal is a psychological defense in which denial and repression are employed to fight off perception of a problem. Withdrawal can lead to serious problems for teens.

In the Sussex study, researchers looked at what they called problem-focused coping and cathartic coping. A teen using a problem-focused coping strategy may express such thoughts as "I try to face my problems head on," or "I ask my family for help." A teen using a cathartic coping strategy may report that, when under stress, "I turn the music up as loud as I can" or "I have a beer or smoke a joint and chill out."

A majority of teenagers believe that smoking relieves stress, so it is not surprising that many of them attempt to use cigarettes in this manner. In fact, teens may start smoking, continue smoking, or return to smoking after having quit in attempts to reduce the stress they feel. The presence of negative emotions of one kind or another is the most common reason teenagers give for lighting up a cigarette. Tensions or conflict at home, pressures at school, and difficulties in peer relationships can all be felt at times as intolerable burdens to adolescents, who then turn to smoking because they believe it will help calm them down, bring on a good mood, or help them cope. Teens also believe that smoking helps them concentrate and many smoke while doing homework or cramming for exams.

According to the experts, teenagers who smoke actually perceive more stress in their lives than nonsmoking teens. Teens in general perceive smoking as an effective coping measure. A large proportion of teenagers are much more likely to use cathartic coping measures (e.g., blasting loud music or throwing themselves into sports) than to use problem-focused smoking strategies. Researchers have found evidence that teens who use cathartic coping strategies are more likely to smoke cigarettes than teens who learn to use problem-focused coping strategies.

The inner psychological lives of teenagers have many similarities but they also have many differences as well. There is no one "teenage personality." Teens are not a homogeneous group. There is no single collective entity known as "teenagers," although adults tend to look at adolescents in that way. Teenagers, and adults, suffer from a range of emotional and physical problems, some of which may contribute to smoking. However, researchers have uncovered some common factors in the way that adolescents view smoking.

As was mentioned earlier, teens see smoking as a pleasurable activity. The immediate pleasurable aspects of smoking outweigh the possible future negative health consequences of smoking. When interviewed by investigators, teens—and adults—reported that they liked playing with lighters and matches; handling the cigarette packs; lighting up and taking the first puff; blowing smoke rings; and many other activities associated with smoking.

Both smokers and nonsmokers, according to the experts, believe that smoking reduces tension, which, in itself, is a form of pleasure. Nonsmokers tend to believe that stress reduction from smoking is a placebo effect; smokers believe it is a direct effect. Cigarette smoking and stress reduction have been so powerfully linked in the public mind that some researchers have found children as young as age eleven who believe that smoking relieves stress. In addition, these young children believed that smoking could help when a person felt sad or depressed. Young children who had tried smoking or who were current smokers said they first picked up a cigarette to see if it would help change their mood. Both children and teens felt smoking could reduce stress when they didn't know how to handle a bully at school, when they had arguments at home, or when they felt pressures at exam time.

Studies show that both nonsmoking and smoking teens know about the dangerous health consequences of cigarette smoking. However, for some teens, the risks associated with smoking are exciting. The possibility of being caught is as exciting to them as the possibility of doing something forbidden and getting away with it.

Teens need to belong and smoking can be a way in which some teens can fit into a group and be part of something. Adolescents who smoke together share a sense of camaraderie that is also found among teens who are on the same athletic team or who are putting on a play at school. Other studies show that smoking is used by some teens as a way to meet members of the opposite sex. An offer of a cigarette can be used as a way to break the ice. Dating and establishing sexual relationships are central aspects of adolescence. Smoking, for some teens, takes the edge off the anxiety they feel about this part of their lives.

The association between body image and smoking is particularly complex. Of course, all teens want to be considered attractive and desirable. It is commonly believed that many girls smoke because they think cigarettes will help keep them thin. The latest research suggests that this may not be the case. Although researchers have found that girls are more concerned about body image, weight, and thinness than boys, recent studies suggest that concerns about thinness and weight may play only a minor role in cigarette smoking among teenage girls. It seems that concerns about weight and attractiveness may not contribute as much to teenage smoking as has been previously thought.

CONTRADICTORY TEEN PERCEPTIONS

Teen attitudes can be contradictory. For example, a number of adolescents surveyed thought that stopping smoking may lead to weight gain. Although they didn't start smoking to keep weight down, these teens were going to continue smoking to avoid weight gain. Many teenage smokers admitted it was better not to smoke, but they believed it was better to be a slim smoker than an overweight nonsmoker.

Adolescent images of smokers and nonsmokers are frequently inconsistent and contradictory. Many teens, investigators have found, are quite ambivalent about how they view smoking. Investigators have interviewed adolescents who have strong positive and negative opinions about smoking and smokers simultaneously. And teenage smokers can have extremely negative images of both smoking and smokers and yet still smoke cigarettes themselves. Some researchers divide teen attitudes on smoking into three categories: psychological, social, and physical. It is this ability to separate out various aspects of smoking in the mind, the researchers suggest, that enables teens to hold contradictory views about smoking.

Researchers have found that teens describe smoking as both a sign of character weakness and character strength. However, more teens view smokers as being "strong" or "tough." Boys who smoke were frequently described as being tough or hard; girls who smoke were also seen as tough. In addition, smokers were thought to be in control, cool, or relaxed. On the other hand, teens also viewed smokers as nervous or under stress and not in control of their lives.

Significantly, adolescents understood that addiction was responsible for excessive cigarette smoking but teens did not associate addiction with adolescent smoking. Addiction, in their minds, was reserved for adult smokers.

Nonsmoking teens generally viewed smoking negatively and described peers who smoked as not very intelligent. The positive images of smoking that adolescents had seemed to come from mass-media portrayals of smokers and cigarettes. Media campaigns portrayed smokers in ways that adolescents desired to see themselves: stylish, classy, successful, attractive, relaxed, accepted, enjoying life. Girls in particular admired the images of the glamorous women in cigarette ads. Both teenage boys and girls thought that smoking enhanced female attractiveness.

Some studies uncovered negative teen images of nonsmokers. Nonsmoking teens were described as being sensible, studious, and obedient. Many teenage boys associated not smoking with a fear of taking risks and of being too attached to parents or other authority figures. Teenage girls often expressed negative views about nonsmoking girls as well. However, researchers found that teens also had positive views of nonsmokers. Frequently, nonsmoking teens were described as being mature or even happy.

In their search to find themselves, teens try on many different identities. Cigarettes can often be a prop used to help create a teen image: the rebel, the outsider, the nonconformist.

For many adolescents, the symbolic aspects of smoking can be far more important than the physical effects they experience from smoking.

The findings of researchers and the experience of professionals who work with teenagers point to the fact that teenage smoking is a phenomenon in which a wide range of factors play important roles. Parents may find that some observations made by the experts apply to their sons or daughters whereas others do not. But the information that has been gathered shows clearly that parents can make a big difference when it comes to helping a teenager stop smoking.

CHAPTER FOUR
What Parents Can Do

Teenagers are frequently able to keep contradictory thoughts about smoking in their minds simultaneously. This mental process allows them to keep engaging in a practice that they know, intellectually, is harmful to them.

In his great novel, *1984,* George Orwell described a process he called "double-think," which involved the ability to believe in two contradictory statements at the same time, as exemplified in the slogan "War Is Peace." In Zen practice, teachers often assign students a *koan* to help them meditate and reach true insight. A koan is an enigmatic statement that puzzles the rational mind, such as "Life is not as it appears; neither is it otherwise." A fundamental piece of advice for parents seeking to help their teenager stop smoking may seem to fall somewhere between double-think and a Zen koan.

This advice could be phrased, "You *can* help your teenager stop smoking; only your teenager can quit." You can be of help to your teen, but each teenage boy or girl must quit smoking on his or her own. This is a difficult task for parents. How can a person help another when there is nothing the person can actually *directly do* to achieve the desired end? You can teach your teen to drive a car, play a sport, or learn a card game by passing on your knowledge directly. But you cannot teach your son or daughter to stop smoking.

There is an old saying, "The student finds the teacher when he is ready." When your teenager is ready, he or she will make it obvious in one way or another. The difficult task each parent has is to recognize when this occurs and then to be there for the teen. Each adolescent must find his or her own way in life and this applies to stopping smoking as well—only the teenager can do the work. But each parent can help guide his or her son or daughter along the way.

The importance of teens doing it themselves cannot be over-estimated. They have to want to quit smoking—to *really* want it. To use the language of the twelve-step programs, teens have to "hit bottom" and be sick of smoking. Popular culture is filled with the image of the romantic, rebellious teenager, from the movie *Rebel Without a Cause* to *Titanic*. Each parent has experienced that moment, a turning point in family life, when a young son or daughter first rebelled and officially became a teenager. However, the energy of this adolescent romanticism and rebellion—which is cleverly exploited by Big Tobacco—is the same energy that can be directed toward quitting smoking. The powerful energy that drives teens to seek independence, to take risks, to want to find themselves, can be redirected and used as a powerful tool help them quit smoking—when they are ready.

It is possible to quit smoking, but it isn't easy. Estimates are that about 30 million people in the United States have quit smoking. It usually takes about four or five attempts at quitting before a person is successful. The various U.S. Surgeons General were not exaggerating over the years when they compared nicotine addiction with heroin addiction. In fact, it is quite common for people to be able to get off heroin but not be able to stop smoking. The evidence shows that the majority of smokers quit "cold turkey." However, this is not the only way to go. Today, there are many smoking cessation programs available to help teenagers and adults stop smoking.

One of the best pieces of advice parents can give their teens when they are struggling to stop smoking is recommended by many experts. (It is actually excellent advice for anyone at anytime.) *Be good to yourself. Treat yourself well.*

EACH TEEN IS AN INDIVIDUAL

Perhaps the most important message for parents to give their teens is "Find your way. Find what works for you." There are diverse ways of stopping smoking. And they all have varying success rates. Parents can help by learning about the various smoking cessation programs. Some programs have great short-term success rates, but do not produce impressive long-term results. Other programs may have lower success rates overall, but in the long run, those who quit, stay quit. Parents can share this knowledge with their teens at the appropriate time.

For each teenager, it is a difficult road from the first daring puff on a cigarette, through regular smoking and bouts of heavy smoking, to a desire to quit and subsequent failed attempts at quitting. It takes a great deal of courage and persistence on the part of a teen to quit. And it can be frustrating, for both parent and teen, when the smoker relapses. However, at some point, your teenager will feel an intense desire to stop smoking, and if you are ready, you can be of help.

What do the words *if you are ready* actually mean? A parent needs to be prepared, intellectually and emotionally, for the moment when a son or daughter wants to stop smoking. As one teen interviewed for this book said, "We need our parents' love and we need them to share with us what they have learned."

The unconditional love a parent has for a child is essential to helping a teen stop smoking. This is not easy for parents to do amidst the frustrations of daily life—earning a living, maintaining a household, caring for other children, and having time for each other. It takes time to be there for a teen, and in today's hectic world in which both parents frequently need to work, time is in short supply.

SMOKING AND OTHER LIFE PROBLEMS

One counselor who works with teens said, "It is so important for parents to take the time to support kids. This can really help them not smoke, not drink, or not use drugs. Tobacco use often masks strong emotions, such as anger or feelings of rejection." Researchers have found that many teens smoke as a way of coping with difficult emotions. "If parents don't take the time," the counselor continued, "kids can feel rejected. In my work with teens, feelings of rejection by parents is a constant theme. Teens will say their parents reject them because they are stupid or because they are bad. For many kids, these feeling of rejection are very intense." To fill this void, teens turn to groups of peers. Some find groups that have a positive impact on their lives, others associate with peer groups that have a negative impact. The research indicates that children who are rejected by their parents—or who *feel rejected* by their parents—have a great deal of difficulty in later years.

It is important for parents to separate teen smoking from the teen smoker. Teens need to know that they are loved and supported even though they are smoking; that despite the ups and downs and frustrations involved in their attempts to quit, their parents are really there for them. This is what is meant by the term *unconditional love.*

Counselors who work with teens have also observed that difficulty dealing with anger affects teen smoking. "Fighting at home," one professional said, "over curfews, grades, school work, or other issues can be very difficult for teens to handle." Frequently, smoking seems like an answer to the anger that it is difficult for an adolescent to express.

Teenage sexuality is a difficult matter for both parents and teens. In our society, we still have not accepted that healthy, natural teenage sexuality is at the center of adolescence. It is often difficult for parents to affirm this basic part of all children's natural development. We are caught between advocating abstinence for moral reasons or half-heartedly tolerating the reality of teenage sexuality. We offer teens sex education, teach them about sexually transmitted diseases, and provide information on contraception—and then hope for the best. Why are so many parents so uncomfortable with the very life function that brought us into existence?

"Teens I work with wonder 'Am I ready?' or 'If I do this, will

I get pregnant?'" a counselor said. "They express their fears and concerns. They have a lot of questions and are looking for answers. Lots of kids may seem advanced in terms of sex today and most kids know some basic information about sexuality. They are very curious. But many are still not ready. Even though they are not ready, kids are under tremendous pressure to be sexually active. Parents need to be aware of this."

The worries and confusion over sexuality are very disturbing to many teenagers. In addition, sexually active teenagers experience an entirely different set of emotional concerns and

WHAT PARENTS CAN DO

1. Learn what resources are available.
2. Learn what the success rates are for different programs and products.
3. Listen empathetically to your teens.
4. Learn to identify with what your teenager is feeling.
5. Keep the lines of communication open.
6. Separate the smoker from the smoking.
7. Respect your teen's autonomy and identity.
8. Create a supportive environment at home.
9. Be there for your teen throughout the whole process of stopping smoking, including relapse.
10. Let your teenager find his or her own way, guiding where you can.

anxieties—STDs, AIDS, and pregnancy, for example. Too often, adolescents have no one to turn to, or are incapable of asking for help. In such situations, lighting up a cigarette may seem to provide at least momentary relief from the stresses they feel.

"A majority of parents don't talk to their kids about sex," a high school counselor said. "In our talks, teens can be more open. We have a policy of complete confidentiality that applies to everything a teen tell us. The only exceptions are threats of self-harm or of harm to others." The irony of this situation is that although parents do not communicate with their children about sex, Big Tobacco does—and does it extremely effectively. "The tobacco ads exploit the sexuality of kids," the counselor continued. "If parents are uncomfortable talking with their kids about certain topics, perhaps they can enlist the help of older siblings."

STYLES OF COMMUNICATING

One of the truly great crimes of Big Tobacco is that, through its advertising and other promotional activities, the industry knowingly takes the powerful Life Energy of adolescents, which naturally expresses itself as love, and redirects it and exploits it to addict teens to their lethal product. Parents can help counteract the influence of Big Tobacco over their teens by communicating with them.

"Parents use a variety of communication styles when talking with their kids," a professional who works with teens said. "Unfortunately, some chastise their kids about smoking. Others talk down to their kids. Most likely, these kids will go on to rebel and start smoking or drinking alcohol. Usually, only rebellion results from lecturing kids."

The psychologist Carl Rogers developed a technique that can be very useful for parents. It is called Empathetic Listening. "The key to parent-teen communication is *listening*," the counselor continued. His observation is supported by research that shows that many teens feel that their parents do not listen to them. "Parents will find Empathetic Listening to be a very helpful tool. It helps you to understand where kids are coming from. And it can prevent you from taking an 'I know better' approach which doesn't really work. I find it helps to start off by being empathetic with kids and *then* set limits." With this approach, real communication between parent and teen is more likely. As a result, parents and teens will enjoy better relationships with one another.

TALKING ABOUT PARENTS' SUBSTANCE USE

Experimentation with sex, drugs, and drinking was quite common when many of today's parents were teenagers. And social attitudes toward smoking were extremely different from what they are today. For some parents, this presents a problem. Many feel reluctant to warn their teenagers about the dangers of behaviors they once engaged in—and probably even enjoyed. In fact, quite a few parents have been confronted by their own children and asked blunt questions about their use of marijuana or other drugs and even about their sexual behavior. How should a parent respond?

"I find that kids respect parents who are honest with them," a counselor said. Of course, parents will have to tailor their answers to fit the individual circumstances of their own family life, the maturity and age of their children, and their own comfort levels. But a reasoned honesty seems a good policy.

"Parents can explain to their kids that the whole zeitgeist—the whole atmosphere of society—was very different in the sixties and seventies," the counselor continued. "We didn't have AIDS; there were fewer STDs; we didn't know as much about tobacco, alcohol, and drugs then as we do today. Parents can tell their teens, 'Yes, we did that but there were *consequences*.' Research shows that teens identify smokers as people who "like to party." Parents can make sure that their adolescents understand that many of the "party people" of their generation suffered from their excessive use and abuse of substances, such as tobacco, alcohol, and drugs. Many of them did not live to enjoy their lives fully.

Risky teenage behavior presents a true dilemma for parents. Teenagers need to learn to make decisions for themselves. Yet parents often want to tell their kids what to do so they won't make mistakes. Another counselor interviewed for this book, a woman with extensive experience working with teenagers, advised, "Don't preach. Adolescents who experiment are often healthier than both those who are afraid to take risks and those who turn to abuse of substances or high-risk sexual behavior. Experimenting is part of being a teen."

The idea that teens who take risks may be psychologically healthier than both those who fear to take risks or those who take too many risks, was put forward in a paper published in the journal *American Psychologist* in the early 1990s. Much practical experience confirms the data put forward by those researchers.

THE POWER OF EMPATHY

In addition to learning to become empathetic listeners, parents can develop another skill that will help them to help their teens stop smoking. One counselor finds it can be very useful to ask parents to "Flash back to your own adolescence. The developmental stages you went through are the same ones your son or daughter is going through. The emotions you experienced then are the same ones your teen is feeling now. In addition to empathetic listening, parents who can feel empathetic identification with their children can really help them."

Adults can learn to identify with their children's feelings. Too often, adults look at teen behavior and think, "I never did that," or "I never said that to my parents." Adults compare their lives and earlier behavior with those of their children. It is more helpful instead to identify with the emotions a son or daughter is experiencing, to identify with the feelings that are motivating a teenager's actions, than it is to compare the details of your life with theirs. Many times, the emotions affecting teens are repressed. Teenagers are frequently unaware that it is repressed anger or fear that is pushing them to reach for a cigarette or a drink or a drug. But a parent who is present, who is really listening to and looking at her teen, can sense what is going on.

"All teenage issues are interconnected," a high school counselor said. "Cigarettes and alcohol and drugs are symptoms of other problems. The schools can't handle this. Kids need their parents to tell them what their experiences have been," the counselor continued. "Teens need this knowledge so that they can use it to help themselves make their own decisions."

A number of teens interviewed expressed clearly how important communication—or the lack of it—with their parents was to them. A fifteen-year-old girl said, "Friends tell each other how their parents don't know how to speak to them. Parents need to pay more attention. Teens need understanding and love. Parents need to communicate." A young woman, a junior in high school, put it succinctly: "Parents need to talk to teens as mature people, but not as adults." Parents will be more successful helping their teens stop smoking if they learn to *mentor, not monitor; guide, don't chide; partner, not preach.*

Two Aspects of Addiction

Youngsters learn to smoke. The research is clear that cigarette smoking is a learned pleasure. At first, smoking is an unnatural act. But then the body comes to want and need the effect of nicotine on the nervous system. The mechanism is similar to that at work with cocaine and morphine. The dependence and later addiction that teen smokers develop keeps them coming back even when they want to quit.

There are two aspects of addiction parents ought to be aware of: psychological addiction and physical addiction. The sensory stimuli from the mental and physical components of smoking play key roles in the development of dependence and addiction. Psychological addiction is intimately interwoven with an individual's lifestyle. Certain things gradually become triggers for a desire to smoke. Negative life situations that produce stress can cause a person to reach for a smoke, such as a problem at work or at school. But positive situations can bring on a desire for a cigarette as well. Movies are filled with scenes of people lighting up a cigarette in bed after making love. A number of the teens interviewed were sexually active and reported that they loved having a cigarette after sex. There is an almost Pavlovian conditioning involved, as people learn to associate smoking with recurring, everyday life situations or moods.

Then there is physical addiction. Nicotine produces its jolt or rush because it has a powerful effect on the nervous system. The nerve endings and the brain cells become used to the feeling nicotine produces. At first, a physical dependence on nicotine develops. This is followed after a period of time by full-blown nicotine addiction. This addiction can be so profound that people who have developed cancer and had laryngectomies—and who now breathe through a hole in their throats—continue to smoke through those surgical breathing holes. In less dramatic fashion, teens who become addicted continue to smoke even when doing so makes them feel bad.

An adolescent who is addicted to cigarettes is really in a tough place. Parents need to keep this in mind as their child struggles to stop smoking.

Once the internal psychological and physical mechanisms of dependence and addiction are in place, providing the internal motivations to smoke, Big Tobacco uses powerful external triggers in the form of slick, high-impact advertising that reinforce the teen's desires to smoke. Big Tobacco also sponsors sports and music events that attract teens. These promotional activities also help reinforce the teen's urge to smoke.

It is difficult to counter these messages in the mass media. One study in *The New England Journal of Medicine* showed that there was less truthful information about smoking in newspapers and magazines that carried cigarette advertising. Publications with no tobacco ads had twice the amount of information as those with cigarette ads. And the greater the number of such ads, the less information there was on smoking. Big Tobacco money is effective in keeping the truth hidden.

Obstacles to Quitting

The first step an adolescent makes in stopping smoking may seem too obvious to mention—the decision to quit. However, the decision to quit may have been preceded by many "decisions" to quit smoking. As Mark Twain said, "Quitting smoking is easy. I've done it a thousand times."

Both parents and teens will be extremely happy with this

wise decision. But forewarned is forearmed. Parents should definitely be completely supportive of their teen outwardly, but inwardly may want to temper their enthusiasm. The process of stopping smoking often involves relapse. A teen may start smoking again because of an event that stirred strong emotions. It could be a positive or negative occurrence, major or minor, internal or external. But relapse is very common. Parents can be there for their child when this occurs and help them to start over again as soon as possible.

There are many obstacles to successfully stopping smoking. Teen fear of failure must be overcome in many cases. Parental support and encouragement is valuable here. They can help teens see that if there is anything to fear, it is the damage caused by smoking. Teens can be reminded that they may have to make a number of attempts at stopping before they succeed. Just as they had to learn how to smoke, they now have to learn how not to smoke.

Some teenagers, particularly girls, fear that they will put on a lot of weight when they stop smoking. Again, parents can allay these fears. Most people who quit smoking put on very little weight. Teens can be reminded that they can lose any weight they may gain. But they lose a lot more by continuing to smoke—and gain so much more by quitting.

Teens who believe that smoking is helping them cope with stress or improving their concentration and ability to do schoolwork may be reluctant to give up their crutch. Teens need to know that they will have so much more energy when they quit smoking that they will be better able to do schoolwork. With increased vitality, they will naturally want to be more active and this physical and emotional activity will greatly help reduce the stress they feel.

Some teens may have heard exaggerated tales of the horrors of nicotine withdrawal and this may cause them to resist stopping. Parents can help by giving them a realistic assessment of what is involved. There is some discomfort; there is no denying that. And it lasts for varying amounts of time. But it cannot compare with the negative consequences of continuing to smoke, consequences that only grow more serious over time.

Paradoxically, smoking has both stimulating and tranquilizing effects. Nicotine is a powerful drug and can produce heavy withdrawal symptoms—irritability, temper outbursts, uncontrollable weeping, anxiety reactions. Parents will have to just ride these out with their teens. The body returns to a normal physiological state but the period of withdrawal varies from person to person. Some people feel fine after only a few days; for others, withdrawal symptoms may last for a number of weeks or even a few months. For many smokers, the psychological addiction may last much longer than the physical addiction.

THE FIRST DAYS ARE THE HARDEST DAYS

Parents can help their teens in the early days of stopping smoking by noticing and commenting on the many benefits of quitting that begin to appear almost immediately: increased energy; improved mood; better breathing; a more confident demeanor.

Some of the improvements are brought about by the absence of the odor of cigarette smoke on hair, skin, and clothing; yellowing of teeth and fingernails; a nagging hacking cough; coughing up phlegm; and the premature wrinkling of skin from smoke. It is difficult to stay off cigarettes so positive reinforcement can strengthen a teen's resolve to stay quit.

Some smokers experience bouts of anxiety and depression after they quit. These episodes are usually mild and they do not last long. Depression during withdrawal from smoking can usually be distinguished from clinical depression, which needs medical attention, because it is less intense and it passes on its own. However, in some teens, smoking may be covering up a preexisting depression that does need treatment.

After quitting, a good number of people find that they crave sweets. Parents can help by having a supply of fruits that teens enjoy around the house. The fructose in fruit is a better way to satisfy the craving for sugar than consuming white sugar products. This is especially true for teens who may be concerned about weight gain. If a teen who is worried about being heavy puts on a few pounds, this could lead to relapse. In addition to eating fruit, teens can kill the craving for sugar by increasing their physical activity. Exercise not only will diminish the desire for sweets, but it will also increase energy, improve mood, tone the body, and keep weight off. And exercise is a good way to ward off the mild anxiety and depression that may occur in the initial period of quitting the habit.

In addition to being strongly motivated to quit, teens need to make a good plan for themselves. Parents can be particularly helpful here. There will most likely be a period of trial and error in which a teen finds what works for him or her. A sixteen-year-old boy interviewed for the book said, "I'd been thinking of quitting for a while. No good was coming from smoking. My friends were all on my back about it. It didn't relieve any tension. I had just had it with smoking." This teen didn't ask anyone for help. He didn't feel he could turn to his parents because they both smoked heavily. "My first attempt was a failure. I tried about four or five times after that. I tried going cold turkey. I tried gradually cutting down but I was soon smoking again. I'd tell myself that I'd quit after this pack. But I didn't."

The young man said he was currently dating a girl he liked very much and was thinking of quitting again. "Girls don't like smoking and she has mood swings when I smoke. She hates the smell and the bad breath." If this young man had parents who were there for him—even parents who smoke can help their teens—he might have been able to design an effective plan and successfully stop smoking. Instead, he is struggling and floundering on his own.

There is no one secret to quitting successfully. There is no single magic formula that is guaranteed to work for all teens. But preparing well for the task can go a long way to ensuring eventual success. Many experts have described the main stages involved in the process of stopping smoking. Some experts have used the following terms to describe those stages: denial, contemplation, action, and maintenance. Parents can use this stages to determine where there teen is in terms of stopping smoking.

When in denial, a teen is not thinking about quitting,

although others may be suggesting it. In the second stage of contemplation, the teenager is thinking about stopping but has not yet come to any decision. At some point in the second stage, the teen makes a decision to quit. This initiates the third stage in which the teen takes action and actually stops smoking. The last stage, maintenance, involves staying off cigarettes for the long term. Parents can be there for their children in all phases of the process and can provide practical help.

THERE ARE CHOICES

There are a number of choices available for those who do not choose to quit cold turkey or who try that method without success. It is important for parents to keep abreast of the latest information on the various smoking cessation products and programs.

NICOTINE GUM

In 1984, nicotine gum was introduced as a way to help smoker's quit. Instead of getting nicotine from a cigarette, the drug was delivered through the gum. This allowed the smoker to wean him or herself off nicotine gradually. It also allowed the smoker to break the powerful psychological connections to smoking by removing the cigarette itself. At first, the gum was only available as a prescription product. In 1996, the FDA approved the sale of nicotine gum as an over-the-counter product.

With these gum products, the nicotine is absorbed through the gums themselves. It is important that teens using these products do not swallow the juice from the gum quickly. The nicotine will not do its job when absorbed through the stomach. The juice needs to remain in the mouth long enough to be absorbed through the gums for it to work. If a teen decides to try this smoking cessation aid, parents should let their child know that certain liquids—coffee, carbonated beverages, and juices—can reduce the absorption of nicotine and the effectiveness of the product. It is important not to smoke when using this product.

Does the gum work? Experts agree that the gum can be effective for a good many smokers. The key to success lies in getting the proper dosage. Research is still being done and the final answer is not in yet.

THE NICOTINE PATCH

In 1992, the nicotine patch came on the market. As with nicotine gum, it was initially available only through a doctor's prescription. This is a powerful nicotine delivery system and there was good reason to require a smoker to visit a doctor to discuss the pros and cons of the patch before beginning to use it. In 1996, the FDA approved the sale of the transdermal nicotine patch as an over-the-counter product. Parents of teens who wish to try this product would be wise to investigate it thoroughly. No one should ever smoke while using the patch. There can be serious problems if they do.

The patch looks like a large bandage. With this system, the nicotine is absorbed directly through the surface of the skin. The nicotine patch delivers a low-level of nicotine to the body over an extended period of time. This helps the smoker wean himself off nicotine. According to the experts, the patch seems to be more effective than the gum for many individuals. A study in *The New England Journal of Medicine* showed that the patch did help people quit smoking. In fact, twice as many smokers using the patch were successful in stopping as compared with a control group that did not use the patch. A similar study conducted in a number of medical centers around the country produced comparable results. This nicotine delivery system continues to be studied.

Although nicotine replacement does seem to lessen the urge to smoke by reducing the craving for nicotine, parents need to know that the patch and the gum are only aids to quitting. In and of themselves, they are not guarantees of success. Each teenager will still have to do the work involved in stopping smoking successfully. The teenager will still need to struggle with the psychological habituation to smoking; the strong emotions that smoking previously masked or helped control; and behavioral patterns that triggered the desire for a cigarette.

Who should use the nicotine patch or nicotine gum? According to the experts, most people can benefit from these products if they are used when the smoker is truly ready to quit. The research suggests that these products may double a teen's chances of quitting successfully. However, if a teen has any physical health problems—or if a girl is pregnant—nicotine replacement may not be advisable. A physician should be consulted.

What is the right strength for these products? It is important to follow the manufacturer's instructions carefully. Experts say that most smokers need to use the full-strength patch at the beginning. This delivers 15–22 mg of nicotine to the body daily for four weeks. A weaker patch that delivers 5–14 mg of nicotine daily is used for the next four weeks. If a teen is using the nicotine gum, experts recommend that smokers begin with the 2-mg dose. However, a 4-mg dose may be required if a teen has been smoking twenty or more cigarettes a day; smoking on waking; having severe withdrawal symptoms; or has been unsuccessful quitting using a lower dose. Light smokers, or individuals with health problems, should talk to a health-care provider for assistance in finding the right dose.

Is either the gum or the patch better? The evidence shows that both smoking cessation aids help. It is a matter of individual choice. Some teens may not like to chew gum throughout the day. Or they may dislike the taste of the gum. On the other hand, some people prefer the gum to the patch. A comparison of what is involved may help parents advise their teenager.

A new patch must be put on the body between the neck and the waist each day. A different spot must be used to avoid skin irritation. The patch is usually used for eight weeks. The gum must be chewed throughout the day in a special way for it to work. It is chewed slowly at first until a peppery kind of taste comes out. Then the teen must position the nicotine gum between the cheek and the gums. Each piece of gum needs to be used for about thirty minutes; a new piece of gum should be used every one to two hours. To work, the gum should be used for anywhere from four to twelve weeks.

The nicotine patch may produce rashes in some people. But they are usually mild and easily treated. Moving the patch around usually helps solve the problem. Some individuals who use the nicotine gum experience upset stomachs, jaw aches, or hiccups. Most of these side effects disappear when the gum is chewed properly.

OTHER SMOKING CESSATION PRODUCTS

Recently, the FDA approved a nicotine nasal spray for use in the United States. It may become an important smoking cessation aid. Much still remains to be learned about the effectiveness of this product as researchers investigate the results people are getting through its use.

In addition, pharmaceutical companies are working on drugs that may be effective in helping people quit smoking. One product is now on the market and is heavily advertised on television and in print. However, it is always wise to be cautious when a new drug is introduced, especially today when the FDA is approving new drugs at an unheard of rate. All powerful prescription drugs have serious potential side effects. In general, the serious side effects of approved drugs do not show up until the product is on the market and many people begin using it.

Clinical trials usually do not involve large enough numbers of people for most side effects to appear. And since clinical trials are conducted with adults, almost always males, the results may not always be applicable to teenagers, especially teenage girls. When considering a drug as part of a teen's attempt to quit smoking, parents should give some thought to the possibility that they may be promoting an attitude of "a pill for every ill." For some teens, this may be counterproductive. The gum and the patch replace the nicotine found in cigarettes, gradually weaning a person off physical dependence. Pharmaceuticals operate in an entirely different way. At this point, it may be more prudent to wait for more evidence to come in about drugs that are promoted as aids to stopping smoking. A physician should be consulted for more information about such products and their possible use.

Weaning off nicotine through use of the patch and the gum seems to work. However, weaning off nicotine by switching to low-nicotine cigarettes does not work. Such cigarettes are nothing more than a clever ploy by Big Tobacco. Many studies show that smokers who switch gain no health benefits and are no closer to stopping smoking. Switching to cigarettes with less nicotine doesn't reduce any of the risks of smoking and doesn't make it any easier to quit.

Some teens try to wean themselves off smoking by lighting up fewer and fewer cigarettes each day. Although this does not work for most smokers, it does seem to help some. A teen may want to give it a try and see what happens. Parents can help by giving their kids a few tips from the experts. For example, don't

Did You Know . . .

🚬 David Goerlitz—the Winston Man—gave up his lucrative modeling career, quit smoking, and works to help teens stop smoking.

🚬 Patrick Reynolds, the grandson of the founder of the R. J. Reynolds tobacco company, quit after ten years of trying and now devotes a great deal of money to helping people quit smoking.

🚬 Of the 14,503 stores permitted to sell tobacco in New York City, since 1993, only thirty stores have been hit with one-year suspensions for selling cigarettes to teens.

🚬 Teen smoking has increased by nearly one-third since 1991 and many health officials blame tobacco industry ads for the rise.

🚬 For 14 months, the State of California ran hard-hitting anti-smoking TV ads and cigarette consumption dropped by 12 percent during that period.

🚬 The ad campaign using Joe Camel increased Camel cigarettes' share of the teen market by 64 percent.

🚬 Half of all people who have ever smoked have quit.

🚬 Eight out of ten teenage boys don't want to date a girl who smokes. Seven out of ten teenage girls don't want to date a boy who smokes. And about 75 percent of teenagers don't smoke.

just smoke fewer cigarettes; gradually smoke less and less of each individual cigarette. Try to catch yourself when you are lighting up without thinking. When you start to light up, hold off for a while. The impulse may pass. Take fewer puffs from each cigarette. Encourage and challenge teens to come up with their own reduction strategies.

HELPFUL ACTIVITIES

Teens can also substitute other activities for smoking. The chewing gum companies have caught on to this and many run effective television commercials presenting gum chewing as a way to fight the craving for a cigarette. Some people try to use fake cigarettes to help them with the psychological aspects of smoking. However, using a fake cigarette may too closely mimic actually smoking and this leads many to just reach for a real cigarette sooner or later.

Exercise and diet can be extremely useful in helping a teen stop smoking. Exercise increases vitality, improves mood, boosts self-confidence, and helps a person breathe better. Exercise also reduces stress and tension far more effectively than smoking. And exercise can be extremely pleasurable and this pleasure can replace the pleasure a teen derives from smoking. In addition, exercise controls weight, answering a concern of teens who fear to stop smoking because they fear becoming overweight. Even moderate exercise is enough to do the trick.

Good smoking cessation programs include exercise as part

of their regimen. This is particularly helpful for teens, who are bundles of energy to begin with. Exercise doesn't mean only boring calisthenics or serious workouts in a gym. Dancing, hiking, swimming, skiing, tennis, volleyball, basketball, soccer, and many other activities teens enjoy can all be of great value in helping an adolescent stop smoking. Again, the pleasure involved in these activities can easily replace the pleasure gained from smoking. If a teen is out of shape, it is important to get back into shape gradually.

DIET AND QUITTING

Teen eating habits frustrate many parents. But parents can help their teens stop smoking by recommending a few simple diet and nutrition tips from the experts. Fruits and vegetables are great helps when a person is stopping smoking. Plan tasty, healthy snacks teens can munch on when cravings for a cigarette arise. For example, chop up fruits and vegetable into bite-sized, ready-to-eat portions and have them readily available. Teens should drink water before meals and throughout the day at this time. Fried foods should be avoided. Broiling, baking, or boiling foods is a better way to prepare them for someone who is quitting smoking.

In addition to the more familiar smoking cessation programs, there are some alternative or complementary approaches that are gaining in popularity. Among them are acupuncture and hypnosis. Acupuncture is an ancient technique that has been used in Chinese medicine for thousands of years. It has become much more acceptable in the U.S. in recent years. In fact, many HMOs are now covering payments for acupuncture sessions. There is some evidence that acupuncture treatments may reduce nicotine craving. Acupuncture may also help minimize the depression, anxiety, and irritability many people experience during nicotine withdrawal. Acupuncture is often used to bring on a relaxed state and has been shown to help with sleep disturbances. Parents should always check the credentials of an acupuncturist to make sure he or she is reputable. In addition, only go to an acupuncturist who uses disposable needles. The use of disposable needles eliminates various health risks, such as the transmission of AIDS through needle sharing.

Hypnosis has been helpful to some people who want to stop smoking but the quality of hypnotists varies widely. There are a number of studies that show that hypnosis, either individually or in groups, produces good success rates. However, parents must be good, informed consumers in this area. Self-hypnosis techniques can also be useful. A professional can teach teenagers how to help themselves through simple hypnotic techniques. Not all experts agree on the usefulness of hypnosis, however. In addition, there are a wide range of relaxation techniques that parents can investigate. If they seem of value, parents can let teens know about them and so they can look into it for themselves.

Parents can provide a great service by helping their sons and daughters develop their own quit smoking plans. To do this, parents need to learn what is out there for their teens and to investigate those options to see which ones offer benefit.

Parents who want to help their teenagers stop smoking face a very difficult battle. Big Tobacco has powerful lies and illusions on its side. They have studied your teenager thoroughly and shaped their message to appeal to the goals, hopes, and desires of young people. It is not an exaggeration to see in tobacco advertising the application of Adolf Hitler's principle of the Big Lie. Hitler understood that it is easier for a Big Lie to be believed than a small lie if the Big Lie is repeated often enough. Tobacco advertising repeats its Big Lie thousands of times a day all over the country and has done so for decades. But this is a battle you and your child can win. Never forget that. You have truth and reality on your side. And the truth about tobacco and cigarette smoking will help set your teenager free.

CHAPTER FIVE
What Teens Can Do

Now it's time to roll up your sleeves and get to work. Do you remember the near-Zen saying from the last chapter, "You can help your teen to stop smoking, but only your teen can quit"? This is the chapter to turn to when your son or daughter has decided it's time to stop smoking and has talked to you about it. The moment of opportunity to be of help is at hand when your daughter or son announces that she or he is determined to quit smoking.

Just about all smokers reach a point when they want to quit. Even Steven F. Goldstone, the Chairman and Chief Executive Officer of RJR Nabisco—which owns R. J. Reynolds, the second-largest tobacco company in the U.S.—reached a rendezvous with his smoking destiny. He quit smoking twenty years ago—yet continues to sell cigarettes to your children today. Goldstone was quoted in *The New York Times Magazine* on June 21, 1998, as saying, "At some point I just said, 'Jeez, I'm killing myself,' so I stopped." The Big Tobacco CEO, the industry's major strategist, further explained. "The pleasure component was beginning to be outweighed by my anxiety that I was injuring my health." These words were spoken by the same Steven F. Goldstone who, along with six other Big Tobacco executives, stood before the House Commerce Committee in January 1994 and raised his right hand to testify that he believed that nicotine was not an addictive drug.

Dr. David Kessler, then FDA Commissioner, told the same House committee that 90 percent of adult smokers picked up their habit by age eighteen. Big Tobacco has tried to present smoking as an issue of "adult choice" and the industry uses its vast wealth to promote "freedom of choice" lobbying campaigns around the nation through bogus front organizations. In contrast, physicians such as Dr. Kessler and former U.S. Surgeon General, Dr. C. Everett Koop, more correctly portray smoking not as a matter of choice, but as a "pediatric disease." Smoking is truly a major issue in child and adolescent health and is finally being portrayed as such.

Parents can help teens put the powerful energy of their desire to quit smoking to good use by providing them with practical information that teens can put into action. There are many smoking cessation methods and programs that have some degree of success. Parents can help their teens learn about these programs and choose among them.

HOW MANY CIGARETTES HAVE YOU SMOKED?

If you smoke a pack a day, you smoke *7,300 cigarettes* each year.

If you have smoked a pack a day for two years, you have smoked *14,600 cigarettes.*

If you have smoked a pack a day for five years, you have smoked *36,500 cigarettes.*

FINDING ONE'S OWN WAY

The most important thing parents can do is to help their daughters and sons *to find their own way.* It is easy to issue orders and make demands on children to obey; it is much more difficult to be a guide. It is easy to tell someone exactly how to do

ARE YOU READY TO QUIT?

Answer Yes or No:

1. Is quitting smoking my top priority?
2. Am I quitting for myself?
3. Have I attempted to quit before?
4. Is smoking dangerous to my health?
5. Am I committed to quitting no matter how tough it may be?
6. Are my family, friends, and peers willing to help?
7. Do I have reasons besides my health that make me want to quit?
8. Do I know what to do when I feel a strong urge to smoke?

(If you answer "yes" to four or more questions, you are probably ready to quit. If you answer "yes" to fewer than four questions, you may need to do more work before attempting to quit.)

something; it is much harder to be there as a support when your child struggles in this difficult effort. Yet, each teenager's struggle to quit smoking is an essential part of quitting. It cannot be avoided or evaded through some short-cut. Each teenager will have to confront his or her smoking head on and take the actions that best help him or her to quit.

Quitting smoking is not a single action. *It is a process.* And it is a process in which temporary failures—or relapse—play an integral role. Parents who help their teens understand *the process of quitting*—the ebb and flow, the progress and setbacks—give their children a great insight. Understanding the process can help teens overcome their fears about trying to quit because of fear of failing, as well as prevent teens who do relapse from becoming so discouraged that they don't try again.

Perfection plays no role in quitting smoking. The process of freeing oneself from the physical addiction and psychological habituation to cigarette smoking is an imperfect, messy process of trial and error. Persistence, not perfection, will pay off. The search for the smoking cessation method that seems best is the beginning of quitting. What follows is information about stopping smoking that your teen can use to create his or her own action plan for quitting.

YOU CAN QUIT SMOKING: ADVICE FROM THE U.S. DEPARTMENT OF HEALTH AND HUMAN SERVICES (HHS)

The U.S. government smoking cessation experts recognize that nicotine is as addictive as heroin or cocaine. Within only a few seconds after puffing on a cigarette, nicotine has made its way into the brain. This causes a cascade of chemicals to be produced by the brain—chemicals that make a person want to smoke. There are powerful physiological forces at play in the body that act to keep a teen smoking even when he or she does not want to smoke.

The first step in the action plan may seem too obvious to mention—but it isn't. It is the decision to quit. When your son or daughter has made this decision, and let you know about it, you are in a position to help. Getting your teen to talk about his

GETTING READY TO QUIT

1. Determine your reasons for quitting; write them down.
2. Try to learn positive lessons from past attempts to quit.
3. Identify obstacles to quitting and devise strategies to overcome them.
4. Know that you can quit successfully; millions of people have.
5. Learn the skills you need to quit successfully.

or her feelings is extremely important, especially about worries and fears. A parent can also provide specific information about cessation programs (e.g., names, phone numbers, addresses) or about quitting strategies. But a parent's help does not need to be direct. You may encourage your teen to speak to a counselor at school or to your family doctor. Today, many health professionals are aware of the hazards of smoking and are prepared to be of assistance. Pediatricians, nurses, dentists, respiratory therapists, physical therapists, and smoking cessation experts are all valuable resources for teens who want to stop smoking. Prepare for the day your teen decides to quit and have a list of names and numbers of people your teen can contact.

SHOULD YOUR TEEN USE SMOKING CESSATION PRODUCTS?

The HHS makes three major smoking cessation recommendations that parents may want to consider suggesting to their teens: (1) using nicotine gum or the nicotine patch; (2) getting support and encouragement; and (3) learning stress-reduction techniques.

All the evidence gathered to date indicates that both nicotine gum and the nicotine patch successfully combat the urge to smoke by reducing the body's craving for nicotine. If your teenager decides to try one of these methods, it is imperative that he or she carefully read the directions on the label or package insert and follow them exactly. Products vary slightly from one to the other. You may want your teen to talk about these products with a physician or other health professional (e.g., a pharmacist) before using them.

Talk to your teen about the patch and the gum. Explain that the scientific studies show that they help almost everyone who uses them. Teenagers need to be honest about how much they are really smoking each day. The dosage from the patch or the gum is determined by the amount of nicotine the body has been taking in from cigarettes. For example, most people start with a 2-mg dose from the nicotine gum. However, if your teen has been smoking more than twenty cigarettes a day, a stronger dosage—4 mg—may be required. Also, your teenager may need a stronger dosage if he or she smokes shortly after waking up, experiences strong withdrawal symptoms, or has previously tried to quit smoking but relapsed. Almost everyone uses the patch at full-strength (15 to 22 mg daily) for four weeks. A second four-week course follows (5 to 14 mg daily).

BENEFITS OF NICOTINE-REDUCTION THERAPY

1. Small amounts of nicotine relieve many withdrawal symptoms.
2. Allows the smoker to break a dependence on cigarettes.
3. It is most beneficial in combination with a good smoking cessation program.

Both products are very helpful. In fact, using either the patch or the gum, in combination with a smoking cessation program, *doubles your teenager's chances of stopping smoking successfully.* It is best to let your son or daughter choose either the gum or the patch, depending on personal preference.

Light smokers or teens with health problems need to talk to a doctor before using either the patch or the gum. Teens who are pregnant, or who think they may be pregnant, should not use either the patch or the gum.

Among the nicotine patch products that are available are Nicoderm (Ciba-Geigy); Habitrol (Aìza Corp./Marion Merrell Dow); ProStep (Elan Corp./American Cyanamid Corp.); and Cygnus Nicotine Patch (Cygnus Therapeutic Systems Inc./Warner-Lambert).

COUNSELING AND
OTHER USEFUL STRATEGIES

In addition to these nicotine-replacement products, teenagers can benefit greatly from the support and encouragement they can receive through counseling. Many studies show that counseling significantly improves your teen's chances of stopping smoking successfully. A limited number of counseling sessions can be extremely valuable for your teen and may even act as a bridge to an appropriate smoking cessation program.

When choosing a smoking cessation program, the HHS suggests that you look for one in which individual sessions are at least twenty to thirty minutes in length; that offers at least four to seven separate sessions; and that lasts for at least two weeks.

You can also help your teen by enlisting the help of other adults (e.g., coaches, teachers) he or she respects and admires; by asking other siblings to show support for their brother or sister; and by asking friends to be encouraging to your son or daughter. In addition, you may want to have self-help material available around the home for your teen, along with any hotline or helpline numbers that are available in your locality.

There will undoubtedly be moments when your daughter or son really wants to have a cigarette. Encourage your teen to make up a list of the names and numbers of people to call when the craving for a cigarette becomes strong and he or she may smoke. Suggest that this list always be with them, at school or at play, for use in an emergency.

Stress can frequently trigger a craving for a cigarette. Most

QUESTIONS TO ASK WHEN CHOOSING A GROUP PROGRAM

1. Is the program conducted at a convenient time and place?
2. Is the professional staff well-trained and experienced?
3. What is the success rate of the program?
4. Does the program meet your needs?
5. What does it cost?

teenagers experience great stress at some time during adolescence; some teens experience a high level of stress throughout this period of life. The HHS strongly recommends that smokers learn about which "people, places, and things" start them thinking about having a cigarette and about relaxation techniques they can use to reduce stress in their lives.

Strong emotions—anger, fear, sadness, loneliness—can all trigger the desire to smoke. Pressures at home and at school can cause frustration that may make your teen reach for a cigarette. Parents who encourage their teens to express their feelings, and who listen empathetically to their sons and daughters, provide invaluable support.

Drinking alcohol is one of the most frequent causes of relapse among people who have stopped smoking. In our society, drinking and smoking go hand in hand. Recent research at the Mayo Clinic shows that people who are addicted to both drinking alcohol and smoking tobacco are far more likely to die from smoking-related disease. According to the Center for Alcohol and Addiction Studies at Brown University in Providence, Rhode Island, lung cancer is a leading cause of death among alcoholics who smoke. All other reasons for not drinking aside, having a beer, a wine cooler, or any other alcoholic beverage may lead your teen right back to smoking.

Parents who learn about relaxation techniques can share this knowledge with their teens. Many young mothers have "Time Out" sessions with their young children. Teens can learn to rely on themselves to call for their own "Time Out" sessions when the craving to smoke occurs. Stress can be minimized by something as simple as sitting quietly for a few moments, breathing regularly, and letting the body slowly relax. This can be done at a desk in a classroom, in the cafeteria, or on the school bus. No one would even notice what the teen was doing.

Pleasurable activities can reduce stress as well. Exercise is a powerful stress-buster. Parents can encourage their teens to get involved with ongoing exercise programs during the period of quitting smoking or to take up physical activity on their own, such as hiking, bicycling, swimming, jogging, or dancing.

Insufficient sleep can both cause stress and decrease a person's ability to handle stress during the day. Parents should keep track of their teens' sleeping habits while they are trying to stop smoking. A good night's sleep is important for everyone, but it is particularly important when a person is trying to tackle a problem as tough as stopping smoking.

Keeping a journal or diary while attempting to quit smoking can also be extremely useful to your son or daughter. In the privacy of a diary, teens can write down how they really feel—angry, frustrated, and doubtful or more energetic, less stressed, and hopeful. Expressing their emotions, getting things off their chests, will relieve a lot of the stress that leads smokers to reach for a cigarette.

Teens who are able to *reach out toward the world*—by engaging in pleasurable activity, expressing their feelings, communicating with others, and asking for help—have an increased chance of success. Parents who help their daughters and sons reach out toward the world do more good than they may ever know.

Finally, parents can help teens devise their own strategies

for quitting. First, support your teen's efforts to set a *Quit Date*. Make an appointment for your teen for a health checkup about two weeks after he or she quits. Encourage your teen to change routines associated with smoking and to throw away ashtrays and other smoking paraphernalia. Suggest that your teen thoroughly air out his or her room to get rid of the cigarette odor. Make sure all clothes are cleaned as well. Help your teen make a new schedule to avoid smoking "triggers" during the day. And, if this is not your daughter's or son's first attempt at quitting, try to learn from the past. Help your teen determine what patterns in thinking and behavior led back to smoking and see if they can be changed or avoided this time around.

FreshStart: 21 Days to Stop Smoking
The American Cancer Society Program

For decades, the American Cancer Society (ACS) has been in the forefront of public education about the dangers of smoking and in offering smoking cessation programs for those who want to quit the deadly habit. The ACS has developed a program that has proven quite effective. FreshStart focuses on the first three weeks of quitting and deals with the three main aspects of getting hooked: physical addiction; psychosocial dependence; and habit. Although the program was designed for adults, the day-by-day technique that is the central element of this program will help your teenager get through the critical first three weeks of stopping smoking.

The ACS focus for teenagers is now more on preventing teens from becoming smokers than it is on smoking cessation efforts. However, since your teen is a smoker who wants to quit, let's look at what the ACS advises. This information can be easily adapted to the needs of your daughter or son.

EVERYONE CAN QUIT

The "one day at a time" approach, which was developed by Alcoholics Anonymous, has been applied successfully by many twelve-step programs around the world. In FreshStart, the ACS employs it to help people quit cigarettes for good, day by day. A basic principle of the program is that *everyone can quit*. It may take a few attempts but everyone can do it. The ACS approach helps the smoker plan for the worst while expecting the best.

Many teens, like all smokers, often want to stop smoking but keep puffing away because it fulfills a need. Parents can help teens by encouraging them to make two lists: "Reasons to Stop Smoking" and "Reasons to Keep Smoking." It can be invaluable to get one's thoughts down on paper and see them before you in black and white. Urge your son or daughter to be completely honest on both lists. After the lists are done, the teen smoker can compare them and see whether he or she is ready to make a commitment to quit or not.

According to the ACS, making a commitment to quitting is the first step in the process. Next comes selecting a Quit Day. When a date has been chosen, the method of quitting is the next

DID YOU KNOW . . .

- Teens become addicted to cigarettes faster than adults.
- The World Health Organization estimates that more than 200 million of today's children and teenagers will be killed by tobacco by 2025.
- From 1992 through 1996, smoking rates among African-American males doubled.
- Lung cancer rates for women have increased over 400 percent in the last twenty years; over 145,000 women die each year from smoking-related disease.
- It is easier for adults to quit smoking than it is for teens.
- The average person gains less than ten pounds after quitting smoking and nicotine gum seems to minimize weight gain.
- Smoking puts babies at risk of Sudden Infant Death syndrome.
- Smoking slows recovery from illness and surgery.
- Big Tobacco needs 5,000 new smokers every day to replace the 1,000 smokers who die from smoking-related disease and the 4,000 who quit or die from other causes.
- Smoking causes 90 percent of lung cancer, 90 percent of emphysema, and 33 percent of heart disease.

order of business. Parents may want to talk to their teens about the various options. "Cold turkey" is the method most frequently used by people who stop smoking successfully. Many teens may want to take this route. However, a teen who has relapsed may be hesitant to go cold turkey. Some teen smokers may want to cut down gradually, tapering off by one or two cigarettes a day until they reach their Quit Day. When tapering off, it is crucial to keep an exact count of how many cigarettes are being smoked so the smoker knows that he or she is actually smoking less.

Others may want to try the technique of "postponing," in which the smoker puts off lighting up that first cigarette for two hours on day one; four hours on day two; eight hours on day three and so forth—until the Quit Day is reached. When using the postponement method, there is no need to count cigarettes. The smoker can have as many cigarettes as he or she wants each

How to Quit

1. *Cold Turkey*: This method provides the best chances for stopping smoking for good. One day you are a smoker, the next day, you're not.
2. *Delay*: Each day, you delay your first cigarette by two hours until you reach a day when you don't smoke at all.
3. *Tapering*: Count the number of cigarettes you smoke, then you keep reducing that number each day until you reach zero.

day after they have started smoking. By starting later and later in the day, the smoker will eventually reach a day with no cigarettes—the Quit Day.

The ACS also recommends that each soon-to-be-ex-smoker do a little bit of "imaging" on that first day. They recommend that the smoker conjure up a vivid, enjoyable image of himself or herself as a successful nonsmoker. In addition, participants in FreshStart are encouraged to write a personal statement that strongly communicates the smoker's desire to quit in only one sentence. The more powerful a sentence, the better. The statement is meant to be seen by the smoker only. It helps greatly to keep the statement in a wallet or purse so it can be looked at in moments of doubt and stress.

QUIT DAY

The day a teen quits smoking may be one of the single-most important days of his or her life. It should be as stress-free a day as possible. Life's problems will rear their ugly heads but parents can assist their teens in creating as stress-free a day as possible. The ACS recommends that each person focus on six items on their quit day: (1) drink enough water; (2) keep a box of cinnamon sticks handy all day; (3) do toe-touching exercises when the urge to smoke hits; (4) practice deep breathing throughout the day; (5) re-read and repeat the personal statement as often as needed; and (6) hold onto the thought of how unique the Quit Day is and what great potential it holds.

Parents can help their teens to follow these ACS suggestions by explaining them. Water helps to speed nicotine out of
the body and to reduce the craving for the drug in most people.
Having a box of cinnamon sticks lets the individual mimic certain smoking-related activities (e.g., holding the stick, suck-
ing on it) and thereby reduces the stress of giving up physical
habits associated with smoking. And exercise is a powerful
stress-buster and can help ward off impulses to smoke.

Deep breathing is very relaxing and is effective in fighting
off the desire to smoke. One young teenage girl, a regular
smoker, who was interviewed for this book, intuited the value
of deep breathing. She said, "I have a theory that smoking is
all about breathing. We want to breathe deeply but we can't. So
we smoke. When we smoke, we breathe deeply, but, unfortunately, we breathe in all these things that are bad for us."

During the day, when the pressures build and the urge to
smoke kicks in, teens can turn to their personal statements for
support. A teen's message to himself or herself can be far more
powerful than a message from another person, whether adults
or peers. In addition, parents can encourage teens to write down
their feelings during the day and describe in words what events
triggered a desire to smoke. By writing things down, teens can
step back, look at their emotions, see how they react to daily
life events, make a connection between these factors, and see
why and when they smoke.

WITHDRAWAL

Physical withdrawal symptoms will be the first big hurdle for your daughter or son. Teens live in the moment and it will be difficult for many of them to think beyond the immediate uncomfortable feelings. According to the ACS, being prepared to face the withdrawal symptoms is the key to getting beyond them. Parents can help by reminding their teens that (1) all withdrawal symptoms disappear with time; (2) the later withdrawal symptoms appear, the weaker they will be; (3) within 10 days, almost all withdrawal symptoms will have passed; all symptoms will be gone within weeks; and (4) each craving lasts no longer than 20 seconds.

Withdrawal symptoms are not signals that something is wrong. They are signs that the body is returning to a state of health. Lightheadedness, headaches, nervousness, tingling sensations in the arms and legs, an increased cough that may be worse than when smoking, and a dry mouth and sense of tightness in the throat are all common withdrawal symptoms. Many people experience mood swings when they stop smoking. Outbursts of anger or sudden bouts of tears are not uncommon. Parents who are aware of these factors can comfort, console, and support their teens.

In this process, it is very important to remember the basics. Teens need to keep drinking enough water, practice deep breathing, exercise, and turn to their personal statements for support throughout the period of quitting smoking.

Relaxation techniques abound today and the shelves of libraries and bookstores are filled with helpful titles, such as *The Relaxation Response* by Herbert Benson, M.D., a pioneer in the field. Progressive Muscle Relaxation (or PMR) is an easy-to-learn and easy-to-practice technique that can fight stress and help ward off the craving for a cigarette. There are many kinds of meditation techniques that are valuable in helping a person handle the stresses that arise when quitting smoking. Teens can be introduced to a whole smorgasbord of relaxation techniques. Most teens will enjoy trying them out to see which ones feel right and which ones work for them. The very process of taking the initiative and finding what works will enhance each teenager's chances of quitting successfully. Parents can help their teens learn about relaxation exercises and encourage their daughters and sons to practice these exercises twice a day for at least fifteen minutes each time.

By the fourth day of not smoking, teens have already helped themselves significantly. Most should be feeling increased energy and vitality. In addition to helping themselves, teens who quit smoking are helping others. For example, parents, brothers, and sisters are all spared exposure to second-hand smoke, a serious problem that results in premature death for thousands of people a year. Also, your teenagers may be surprised to find extra money in their pockets—money formerly handed over to Big Tobacco. All these factors can come up naturally in conversations between parents and teens, reinforcing their resolve to stop smoking for good.

TRIGGERS TO RELAPSE

As the days progress, and physical symptoms begin to subside, it is useful for teens to continue to identify "triggers" that make them think of smoking. The repeated habits associated with smoking need to be identified and broken. These activities are so ordinary your teen may not even think they are linked to smoking. Lighting up a cigarette may go along with a morning coffee, having a beer, doing homework, feeling angry

THE "BENEFITS" OF SMOKING

- Causes rapid heartbeat and high blood pressure.
- Replaces life-giving oxygen with poisonous carbon monoxide.
- Stains fingers and teeth an ugly yellow.
- Weakens muscles and impairs breathing.
- Causes shortness of breath.
- Decreases athletic ability.
- Causes bad breath.
- Leaves a foul odor on hair and clothing.
- Doubles or triples the risk of a heart attack.
- Is the major cause of over 420,000 deaths a year from lung cancer.
- Is the major cause of emphysema and bronchitis.

or lonely. Many teens are sexually active and may smoke after making love.

Talk to your teen about when he or she smokes. Try to get your teen to open up about situations that really make them feel like smoking. Help your daughter or son make the connections between ordinary, everyday habitual behavior and cigarette smoking. Just becoming aware of the connections is helpful. The teen doesn't have to change all of these behaviors. Simply breaking a few behavioral links, along with the diminishing withdrawal symptoms and increasing time away from smoking, will help your teenager stop smoking successfully. Time is a great ally of your son or daughter. Nicotine leaves the body; the withdrawal symptoms gradually subside; "triggers" lose their power; and your teenager will begin to feel better. This improved sense of well-being is a powerful motivator in itself.

Although it is illegal for teenagers to drink in most states, parents know that many teens do drink alcohol. It is extremely difficult for drinkers to stop smoking. Alcohol changes a person's thinking and can easily lead a teen to light up a cigarette. In addition, many teens smoke marijuana, even though it is illegal. Some teens even find that smoking a cigarette increases the marijuana "high." This is very popular in England, less so in the United States. Parents have varying attitudes toward teen drinking and marijuana use, but all parents should be aware that the use of these drugs will make it much more difficult for their teens to quit smoking.

EMOTIONAL HIGHS AND LOWS

As the weeks progress, teens may no longer feel physical symptoms that bother them and they may succeed in breaking the

HOW TO HANDLE
WITHDRAWAL SYMPTOMS

Coughing: Drink lots of water; try warm herbal teas; use lozenges, cough drops, or sugarless candies.

Dizziness/Lightheadedness: Exercise regularly.

Irritability: Relaxation exercises, such as deep breathing, hot baths, physical activity.

Constipation: Drink six to eight glasses of water a day; eat plenty of whole grains, raw vegetables, and fruits.

Fatigue/Tiredness: Daytime naps; sleep longer at night; eat properly; keep active.

Nicotine Cravings: Relaxation exercises; count to ten and craving will pass; call a family member or friend; remember the craving will pass.

Sore Throat or Mouth: Sip ice water; chew sugarless gum; rinse sore mouth with warm salt water.

links between certain behaviors and smoking. However, they may begin to experience emotional ups and downs. There may be moments of sudden sobbing or outbursts of laughter. Your teen may be especially irritable. Emotional mood swings are common but, like the physical withdrawal symptoms experienced in the first days of quitting, they will pass.

Your daughter or son may be embarrassed by these mood swings and may need more privacy, especially when he or she needs to cry. This emotional upheaval is perfectly natural. It is a part of the body's struggle to regain a state of balance. In fact, the release of these emotions actually contributes to healing. Your teenager will invariably feel better after expressing these emotions.

Parents can ease their teens' struggles by letting them know that these mood swings are part of the process of quitting smoking. However, in some instances, there may be an underlying problem surfacing now that the cigarettes aren't there to cover up the hidden feelings. Some experts believe that cigarette smoking masks depression in a number of teenagers. If the crying persists, or if there are prolonged periods of sadness, it may be wise to talk to your doctor or counselor. It is very important not to ignore the possibility of depression.

Many teenagers will experience difficulty concentrating and this may make them desire to pick up a cigarette. Most teens—both those who smoke and those who don't smoke—erroneously believe that smoking helps improve concentration. Many teens believe smoking relaxes them and helps them do their homework better and to study harder for exams. The difficulty in concentrating is another physical symptom of withdrawal. Just as the lungs need to adjust to life without cigarette smoke, so too does the brain. The stimulation of nicotine is gone; the excess of carbon monoxide is gone as well. And the brain is receiving more oxygen than it is used to getting. In addition to these physical factors, your daughter or son may be feeling anxious without a cigarette and this also contributes to an inability to concentrate. As with the earlier withdrawal symptoms, this will also pass.

Exercise can help relieve the problem. Taking short breaks from schoolwork will also help your teenager focus once again. If your son or daughter has a big assignment to complete, and a lack of concentration is preventing him or her from working, help him or her divide the task into manageable, bite-size portions that can be completed in stages. A glass of milk can also calm the nerves. Also, there are a number of natural products that may help restore balance and the ability to concentrate. Talk to your doctor, health professional, or pharmacist for advice about these helpful remedies.

Sleep disturbances occur among some who are in the process of quitting smoking. If your teen is having trouble getting up in the morning, try to help him or her get to bed a little earlier for a few weeks. If they are waking up at the crack of dawn, help them devise useful ways to use the extra time they now have. Regular exercise will help fight sleeping disturbances. Deep breathing and other relaxation techniques will also go a long way toward alleviating sleeping problems. Parents can remind their teens of the simple, practical solutions for their problems that exist. And they can reassure their teenagers that the turmoil they are experiencing is only temporary, that it will pass in a matter of days or weeks, and is part of the process of returning to a state of health and vitality.

THE LURE OF SMOKING AGAIN

In the song "Uncle John's Band," the Grateful Dead sing, "When life looks like Easy Street, there is danger at your door." After the difficult initial period of physical and emotional withdrawal from cigarettes, there will be a period of calm and ease. It will all seem so simple. Your teenager may begin to think, "That wasn't so hard. In fact, it was pretty easy." As hard as it is to believe, many people start smoking again just when they begin to achieve some success in quitting. Your daughter or son may think "I can have just one smoke," or "I quit and proved I'm not addicted. Now I can smoke and control my smoking." These types of thoughts frequently lead to relapse.

It is just as important, in the first glow of success, to communicate with teens. Those who have just quit need to continue to open up and express their feelings. They need to examine how they are feeling now that they no longer have to smoke everyday. The illusions of Big Tobacco are out there, as powerful and alluring as ever. There is the illusion of the "social smoker," that is, the person who makes a so-called "adult choice" to inhale over 400 poisonous and lethal chemicals. There is the illusion of the suave, cool and collected smoker. And, of course, there is the potent fantasy of the sexy smoker—the "real" man and

SMOKE GETS IN YOUR EYES

Smoke doesn't just irritate your eyes. Cigarette smoke harms the entire body. Here are some examples of what smoking does to you:

Skin: becomes discolored, leathery, wrinkled.

Muscles: are greatly weakened by smoking; athletic performance reduced.

Mouth/Throat: cigarettes cause bad breath and increase your chances of getting oral cancer.

Bronchial tubes: become irritated and smaller, resulting in chronic bronchitis.

Lungs: self-cleaning ability damaged; breathing capacity lessened; poisonous chemicals from cigarettes can cause lung cancer.

Blood: red blood cells absorb almost all of the carbon monoxide from smoke, causing entire body to get less oxygen; nicotine carried by blood to brain and rest of body.

Blood vessels: nicotine makes blood vessels smaller, contributing to high blood pressure and heart disease.

Brain: decreased oxygen and blood flow to brain from cigarette smoke; brain experiences unpredictable effects, e.g., irritation, depression, relaxation.

Heart: great damage from smoking; more smokers die of cigarette-related heart disease than lung cancer.

Stomach: smoke promotes ulcers, affects digestion negatively.

glamorous supermodel woman—who are so appealing to adolescents just coming into their own sexual maturity.

Parents and teens can analyze the cigarette ads that appear
in newspapers and magazines. It is a good way to defuse them
and make them less powerful. The ads lend themselves to
humorous criticism because the contrast between the images
of sparklingly clean, happy, healthy fun-loving smokers bears
little resemblance to the reality of smoking—smelly clothes
and hair, yellow nails and teeth, dirty ashtrays, a hacking cough,
premature wrinkling, etc.

There is new evidence that cigarette smoking is linked to
impotence in men. Apparently, Big Tobacco has been aware
that cigarette smoking caused sexual problems for men but kept
this hidden. In California, a new series of TV commercials and
billboard ads are highlighting the association of impotence and
cigarette smoking.

Parents can also remind their teens that there is no such
thing as having "just one cigarette." Teens know that their habit
started with just one smoke, but it led to a serious problem, one
that made them unhappy enough to make the difficult effort to
stop smoking. Congratulate your teen for facing a tough problem head on. Celebrate mileposts in quitting—day one, the first
week, one month, and so on. But remind your teen of the effort
it has taken to quit, and of the practical steps to continue taking every day, one day at a time, to stay off cigarettes. Everything your teenager has gained could be jeopardized by a puff
or drag on a friend's cigarette; trying to smoke in a controlled
way; or having just one cigarette on some special occasion.

STAGES OF QUITTING

According to the ACS, there are four stages to quitting smoking: (1) thinking about quitting; (2) making the decision to quit; (3) actually quitting; and (4) staying off cigarettes. By the time a person begins the second week of not smoking, he or she has completed the first three stages. But it is around this time that the craving for a cigarette can try to sneak in the back door through a process called rationalization. When a person rationalizes an action—such as starting to smoke again—a plausible but false reason is given for taking the action. The smoker making the rationalization believes it; many parents and friends may believe it as well. Unless they stop to think a moment.

Don't be surprised if your teen starts to utter such rationalizations as "I've proven I can quit." Parents can help their teens identify such thoughts for themselves. Teens who keep a journal or diary, and who write down their true feelings about smoking and quitting smoking, will see these rationalizations before their own eyes in their own handwriting. Again, communication is the key. Parents who talk to their children—and who listen to them—provide invaluable support. Encourage your sons and daughters to examine what they think about quitting. Help them to identify tricks their minds will play, tricks that will lead back to smoking.

As with habits related to smoking, which were broken one at a time, false ideas can be identified and eliminated one at a time. A teen can write down the rationalizations for smoking again in one column, the reasons for not smoking in a column alongside it, and then compare them. This can be a powerful tool in helping an adolescent stop smoking successfully. Remember, the process of quitting smoking is difficult, but everyone can do it.

The Maryland Division of the American Cancer Society developed a smoking cessation program for young people— The Smoke-Free Teens Program—during the fall of 1992 and tested it out as a pilot project in Baltimore and four counties in Maryland in 1993. It has undergone some revisions and is ongoing today. The Maryland ACS felt that, although there are many good smoking cessation programs in existence, one tailored for teens was needed. The program consists of ten sessions, with each session lasting about forty to forty-five minutes. The goal is to educate teens to make healthful and permanent choices about tobacco use and provide a process and group support for youth to be smoke-free.

The readiness of teens to quit smoking is assessed and teens are taught about tobacco and health. In addition, teens are introduced to life skills that can help them change their behavior. The importance of aftercare is emphasized. In this program, teens enter into a "contract" which guides them in the process of stopping smoking. A manual and other materials were developed to assist facilitators in their work with teens.

This program for young people opens each session with an optional relaxation activity. Various strategies are used to get teens motivated, to focus their energies on quitting. Information is presented to the youngsters, but teenagers are also encouraged to express their feelings and share their thoughts about smoking and quitting smoking with the group. The teenagers are asked to write down why they smoke, what they like about it, how it makes them feel. They are also asked to write a list of reasons they want to quit smoking.

Methods of stopping smoking are introduced and explained. Teens identify smoking-related behavior they want to change and draw up contracts to follow through on putting those changes into effect. The three factors in nicotine addiction—physical addiction, habit smoking, and psychological dependence—are explored. Students brainstorm about these topics, as well as about the health consequences of smoking.

Working with partners or buddies, teens discuss why they want to quit and come up with personal strategies for quitting. The pros and cons of three methods—going cold turkey, delaying smoking, and tapering off—are discussed and explained. Buddies copy down each other's phone numbers and promise to be there to help one another during the process of quitting. Teens are also asked to step forward and publicly throw away all of their smoking paraphernalia such as matches, favorite lighters, and rolling papers.

By the fifth session, teens are exhorted to select a Quit Day. In this program, there is a Quit Day celebration to mark the importance of the occasion. In the following sessions, in an active, participatory format, teenagers look at such subjects as developing coping strategies to deal with giving up cigarettes; devising personal methods of handling stress; learning a variety of relaxation techniques; and sharing with one another what activities worked and did not work for them.

The benefits of being smoke-free and of living healthy are also the subjects for participatory sessions. Nutrition, weight change, exercise, and increased physical activity are discussed in relation to stopping smoking successfully. Teens are helped to develop and maintain a support network while they get unhooked from nicotine. Also, teens learn to devise long-term strategies to stay smoke-free after their participation in the program has ended.

WORKING WITH YOUR TEEN

Parents can use many of these approaches and techniques at home with their teenagers. This is done most effectively by incorporating this information into daily life. There are many opportunities during the week to bring up smoking-related information in casual conversation with your son or daughter. It isn't necessary to have special discussions or to lecture to or teach this information to your teen. Simply by being there for your son or daughter, by communicating, you will have ample opportunity to bring up many of the actions teens can take that are described above.

Relaxation techniques abound today. They can not only help the teen who is trying to get unhooked from cigarettes, they can also be useful to parents and family members who have to deal with the ups and downs of the smoker who is quitting.

Although they are increasing in popularity, many Americans know very little about relaxation exercises. They help reduce stress and bring on a sense of inner peace. For them to work fully, the person using the relaxation technique needs to be willing to become more aware of his or her feelings, experience the natural inner need for tranquillity, and engage in some level of self-reflection and introspection.

Parents and teens can explore a variety of relaxation techniques. Individuals can choose the exercises that work best for

TIPS FOR CONTINUED SUCCESS

- Create a smoke-free environment at home.
- Write down your most important reason for stopping smoking and keep it with you.
- Tell your friends you've quit and ask for their help.
- Don't be overconfident.
- Put the money you would spend on cigarettes and save it. Use this money to treat yourself to things you enjoy.
- Don't carry matches, lighters, or other smoking paraphernalia with you.
- Hang out with people who don't smoke.
- Celebrate your no-smoking anniversaries.
- Reward yourself by treating yourself to a movie, a concert, or dinner with a friend.
- Take pride in the difficult task you are accomplishing.

them. The experts recommend picking a form of relaxation exercise that you really enjoy. Don't choose one because it's popular and everybody is currently doing it. Try something that is completely new and different to you and see how it feels. Enter into this activity with enthusiasm and *joie de vivre.*

Parents can also help their teens by reminding them to perform their relaxation exercises on a daily basis. Parents who practice relaxation exercises themselves can be powers of example and lead by deed, not by word. To stop smoking and stay stopped, it is very important for teens to achieve a sense of balance and calm at regular intervals during the day. Your son or daughter has a wide range of techniques and activities to choose from.

For starters, you may want to look into two simple and easy-to-practice forms of relaxation exercise: deep breathing and muscle relaxation. Both of these exercises will help a person learn to relax at will. They can be used separately or together. To gain the optimum effect, they need to be practiced at least once a day.

For the deep breathing exercise, you stand with feet apart in a comfortable stance and head bent forward slightly. Then let your head drop further. Slowly inhale through the nose, drawing the breath deep into the abdomen. As your abdomen expands, allow your head to rise slowly with inhalation. Then exhale slowly, breathing out through the nose. Repeat this procedure at a pace that is comfortable. If dizziness occurs, simply stop for a few moments until it clears up. Deep breathing can be practiced until a sense of relaxation spreads over the entire body.

With muscle relaxation, try standing with the feet planted

firmly on the ground. This exercise can be done with eyes open or closed, whichever is more comfortable. While breathing slowly, tense your feet. Then increase the tension in your feet. Next, make the tendons and calf muscles tense, and then the thighs. Increase muscle tension up to the abdomen, up to the chest, then all the way up to the shoulders. Make the arms and hands tense and then the neck muscles and the face. Make the scalp tight as well. Hold the body in a state of tension briefly—and then relax. Let the tension slowly drift away. Let the feelings of total relaxation spread over the entire body.

There are many variations of these two relaxation exercises, and many different kinds of relaxation techniques as well. The benefits that they offer will help your teenager during the process of stopping smoking. And they will also benefit you, your spouse, and any other family member or friend who incorporates them into a healthy lifestyle.

Social support is also crucial for teenagers who are trying to stop smoking. Researchers have discovered that people with support from others have greater success in stopping smoking. And people who help a teen quit smoking can play an important role in keeping them away from cigarettes over the long term. Parents, family members, and peers can provide great support for teens. So can the staff at school, roommates at boarding school, coworkers at part-time jobs, and others with whom your son or daughter comes into regular contact. Parents can encourage teens to ask others for help, and be powers of example themselves by supporting their children.

Teenagers concerned about gaining weight after stopping

smoking can take some simple steps to prevent that from happening. They can (1) plan their meals ahead of time; (2) avoid eating too much sugar; (3) keep physically active; (4) avoid snacking on junk food and eat popcorn or raw vegetables instead; and (5) get on a scale and watch their weight each day. If your teen does gain a few pounds, let him know this happens to many smokers and help him develop a plan to shed the unwanted pounds in a sensible manner.

FREEDOM FROM SMOKING

The American Lung Association (ALA) has an excellent smoking cessation program—Freedom from Smoking—and parents and teens can get information and help from this organization. Since 1904, the ALA has been fighting lung disease through research, education, community service, and advocacy.

In its smoking cessation program, the ALA first asks the person considering quitting to be sure he or she really wants to quit. Parents can ask their teens to explain why they want to stop smoking. Some will say, "For my health"; others will respond, "I don't want to smell bad and have my teeth turn yellow"; and still others will reply, "So I'll feel better," or "Smoking is a waste of money." It is important that teens know why they want to quit and that they be determined to quit. As do other programs, the ALA suggests that the smoker write down his or her reasons for quitting.

There may also be mental roadblocks in the way that could

make it difficult or impossible for your teen to stop smoking successfully. By really listening, you can help your teen bring clarity to confused thinking. For example, a teen may not feel confident and say "I don't have the will power to quit," or "All my friends smoke and it'll be too hard for me to quit." By answering these concerns rather than just dismissing them, a parent can help a teen take action. A parent can acknowledge that it is harder to quit when one's friends smoke, but the parent can also show the teen where to find help and support in quitting from other people. Fear may cause a teen to feel that she doesn't have the willpower. Her parent can reassure her that millions of ex-smokers felt that way at the beginning but they took the first step anyway—the decision to quit.

OVERCOMING ROADBLOCKS TO SUCCESS

There are many mental roadblocks in the way for smokers, the rationalizations discussed earlier. Teens need to be listened to when they express fears and concerns about quitting. And they need to be encouraged to express these doubts and to write down their thoughts and concerns. When fears are taken out of the head, and put down on paper, they lose much of their power.

Some teens may not feel they are addicted. The ALA has put together a five-question test, requiring a simple yes or no answer, to determine if a person may be addicted.

1. Do you smoke your first cigarette within thirty minutes of getting up?
2. Do you smoke a pack (twenty cigarettes) or more a day?
3. At times when you can't smoke or don't have a cigarette, do you feel a craving for one?
4. Is it tough to keep from smoking for more than a few hours?
5. When you are sick and in bed, do you still smoke?

If a teen answers "yes" to two or more of the above questions, he may be addicted. The more a teen answers yes, the greater the likelihood of addiction. Such simple tests can help break down a teen's resistance to quitting and denial about the real situation. As with the approaches mentioned earlier, the ALA smoking cessation program emphasizes the importance of preparing to quit; picking a firm Quit Day; planning ahead, especially during the first few weeks of quitting; identifying and breaking old habits that are related to smoking.

In addition, Freedom from Smoking focuses on the importance of getting help from others—parents, siblings, doctors or other health professionals, friends, teachers, coaches, classmates, and coworkers. The ALA stresses that it is important for the person quitting to be specific and tell others exactly how they can help.

The ALA also suggests that the person quitting write a letter to the person she most wants most help from. Parents can recommend that their teens write such a letter and help them shape their thoughts. The ALA offers a model letter that teens

SNUFF OUT SNUFF

In the spring of 1998, 141 major league baseball players volunteered for a cancer screening program run by Dr. John C. Greene, an oral cancer specialist working with the National Spit Tobacco Education Program. Dr. Greene found that 83 players—nearly 60 percent of those tested—had at least one oral lesion related to tobacco. Dr. Greene recommended biopsies for fifteen players to determine if the lesions were cancerous. As many as 300 of the 750 players in the major leagues now use chewing tobacco.

The drive against smokeless tobacco picked up momentum in 1996 when a former major leaguer, Bill Tuttle, visited players during spring training. Mr. Tuttle—who appeared on baseball cards in the 1950s and 1960s with a fat wad of chewing tobacco in his cheek—had chewed tobacco for forty years. He had undergone a series of operations for oral cancer and had lost part of his jaw, a cheek, his taste buds, and some teeth. The young players didn't know the former Major Leaguer but when they saw his face, they were silent and listened to his story. Million-dollar stars came up to him and asked him to throw away their cans of tobacco.

Bill Tuttle died at the age of 69 in July of 1998, after a three-year battle with cancer. It was his dying wish that his smoking education campaign would continue and that it might save others from the great harm smokeless tobacco had caused both him and his family.

can start with and adapt to their own needs. It is suggested that the letter begin with a direct statement such as "I need your help to stop smoking." It is recommended that the letter be positive and specific. Some of the suggestions might be difficult for a teen to write down, but parental support can help them do it. For example, the ALA suggests that teens write "Ask me how things are going from time to time," and "Reward and praise me. Rewards don't have to cost much. It's the thought that counts."

The ALA also recommends making the Quit Day a special day. In addition to getting rid of all cigarettes and smoking paraphernalia, it is highly recommended that the soon-to-be ex-smoker engage in some pleasurable activities, such as going to a movie, taking a long, relaxing bath, eating out in a favorite restaurant, buying a new CD, getting a new hairstyle, attending a ball game or concert, or taking someone out for dinner.

The major aspects of the various smoking cessation programs overlap and don't need to be repeated at this point. If it is not possible for your teen to attend a program such as Freedom from Smoking, the ALA has published an excellent companion book called *7 Steps to a Smoke-Free Life* that you may want to get for your teenager. Although not written specifically for teens, there is valuable information in the book, for both parents and teens.

ASSERTIVENESS TRAINING

One aspect of smoking cessation not discussed yet is assertiveness training. Many parents of teenagers may roll their eyes and moan at the very thought of their sons and daughters becoming more assertive than they already are. However, assertiveness is not the same as being aggressive or rebellious. Often, many rebellious people—teens or otherwise—are not very assertive in standing up for themselves in important life situations. Smoking a cigarette is frequently an effective means of getting rid of the frustration and low self-esteem a person feels when they aren't assertive.

Parents can help teens by talking to them about the differences between being rebellious or aggressive and being assertive. The experts say that an assertive response is controlled, positive, and direct. In contrast, rebellious behavior or aggressive behavior is frequently uncontrolled, negative, and misdirected. An example of an assertive response is expressing your own feelings and your own desires and needs. Aggression usually involves a criticism or attack on another person and a demand that the other person change. To stop smoking successfully, teens need to learn to change themselves, to express their feelings—in other words, to be assertive.

Some teens act in a passive way when the situation calls for an assertive response. This behavior, too, can lead to difficulties when it comes to stopping smoking. Passivity usually leads to and results from low self-esteem. The person's true feelings are repressed and the resulting tension can lead to a desire to smoke.

Many of these behaviors are learned and, fortunately, with some help and guidance, teens can learn new ways of behaving. And these new, assertive ways of behavior will prove immensely useful not only in quitting smoking but also in making one's way in life in general.

A Flexible Program

One of the advantages of the ALA "7 Steps to a Smoke-Free Life" program is that it has no predetermined timetable to it. Your teenager can adapt it to fit her or his own schedule and needs. It's a simple, flexible program. There is no calendar of events that must be accomplished by specific days. As useful as a definite schedule can be for some, it can sometimes become a stumbling block for others. According to the ALA, their program is especially useful for people who have tried to quit before but who have not been successful. Their approach helps the smoker learn positive lessons from past failed attempts. In addition, this format uses a group leader, which is helpful for many people, and offers group support for the person attempting to quit.

With the "7 Step" approach, your teen will learn to ask three basic questions about his or her quitting plan:

"What's the best type of program for you?"

🚬 "What mode of quitting seems best for you?"

🚬 "Do you want to use medications to boost your efforts?"

If your teen wants to try a self-help approach, the ALA book or literature, ACS books or literature, and other useful smoking cessation books now available can all be helpful. If your teen wants to try a group-support approach or a smoking cessation program, consult your local phone directory for the names and numbers of organizations, or contact the ALA, ACS, a local hospital, or YMCA/YWCA to find out what smoking cessation groups are active in your area.

WAYS TO QUIT

As do other programs, the ALA suggests going cold turkey as one method of quitting. They also talk about what they call "nicotine fading," a process of changing the brand of cigarette smoked to gradually reduce nicotine intake before quitting. Not all smoking cessation programs recommend this technique.

Although most smokers do not use medication to assist them in quitting, many find that these products are helpful. Nicotine replacement is possible by using nicotine gum, the nicotine patch, nicotine nasal sprays, or nicotine inhalers. The ALA approach also considers the possible use of hypnosis and acupuncture.

Before using any nicotine-replacement product, your teenager must have stopped smoking completely. Nicotine overdose can result from using these products while smoking; the side effects are quite serious. The nicotine spray was approved by the FDA in 1996 and the nicotine inhaler in 1997. The ALA, like other programs, has found that those who use nicotine-replacement therapy in combination with a good smoking cessation program double their chances of succeeding at quitting.

While the patch and the gum are now available over the counter, the spray and the inhaler are available at present only through a doctor's prescription. These products are not cheap, either. However, they cost far less than a pack-a-day smoker spends on cigarettes. The research shows that people do not become dependent on the nicotine in these products as they did with cigarettes. These products should not be used for more than three to six months. They aren't magical and they don't remove all cravings for nicotine. They are not a panacea, but they do diminish the desire for a cigarette dramatically.

7 STEPS TO A SMOKE-FREE LIFE

1. Understand your habit and addiction.
2. Build your motivation to quit.
3. Develop your quitting plan.
4. Prepare for your Quit Day.
5. QUIT!
6. Learn how to fight temptations.
7. Stay focused on your goal.

The specifics of the patch and the gum were discussed earlier. In the ALA "7 Step" approach, the new nasal spray and inhaler are considered as useful as well, when combined with their program. If you and your teen think these might be helpful, make an appointment with your doctor to discuss the pros and cons. You'll need a doctor's prescription in order to get them. The spray and inhaler cannot be used if your teen is still smoking. And your teen cannot be using any other form of tobacco product.

The nasal spray delivers the nicotine through the membranes in the nostrils. The inhaler delivers nicotine through the mouth. In just minutes, both deliver low amounts of nicotine to the body. How low? Ten puffs on the inhaler equals about one puff on a cigarette. These temporary aids can't do the job by themselves. Even when using a nicotine-replacement product, teens need to continue to keep their motivation levels high, stay physically active, refer to their personal statement about quitting, express their feelings verbally and in writing, and reach out for help.

New nicotine-replacement products will continue to be developed and parents who keep themselves informed can educate their teens about what options are available. In addition to nicotine-replacement therapy, drug companies are creating new medications for people who are quitting smoking. As with nicotine-replacement therapy, opinions vary about the desirability of replacing one drug—nicotine—with another drug.

However, a "new" product has hit the market and is being heavily advertised. It is called Zyban (bupropion hydrochloride). In reality, this product is not new at all. It simply has a new "indication" or use. Previously, bupropion hydrochloride was marketed as an antidepressant and sold under the brand-name of Wellbutrin SR. It is quite common for drug companies to find new uses for old drugs, especially when their patent protection is about to expire. For example, the best-selling drug, Rogaine, was formerly a failed antihypertension medication that found new life being rubbed onto bald spots, and AZT, the drug for AIDS, was a failed anticancer drug that was resurrected to treat a new disease.

Bupropion hydrochloride increases the body's levels of dopamine and norepinephrine, two important chemicals in the brain. Nicotine also boosts the levels of these chemicals. When dopamine and norepinephrine levels are high, people feel energetic and have a strong sense of well-being. The drug ads promise that those who use this product will experience these feelings of well-being and get help quitting smoking on top of that. Early research suggests that the new pill may help some people. And, as with nicotine-replacement products, the drug works best in combination—when used with smoking cessation programs or some other form of professional support. However, parents and teens considering using prescription drugs to help get off a drug may want to exercise caution.

Zyban is taken twice a day, once in the morning and again in the evening. It does not work immediately; effects don't appear for about a week. In contrast to the nicotine patch, gum, spray, and inhaler, the drug must be taken *before an individual quits smoking*. The levels of dopamine and norepinephrine need to be elevated by the time a person quits smoking. The ALA recommends that people using this drug select a Quit Day one to two weeks after they start taking the medication.

Some research suggests that using Zyban beyond an eight-week period does not provide increased benefits. If your teenager uses this drug, and stops smoking for eight weeks, talk to your doctor about plans for weaning him from it.

Zyban isn't for everyone. Both parents and teens need to talk to a doctor about this drug. The drug is not recommended for women who are pregnant or who think they might be pregnant; people suffering from eating disorders (e.g., bulimia or anorexia nervosa); anyone taking an MAO inhibitor for depression; anyone taking Wellbutrin, Wellbutrin SR, or other medications containing bupropion hydrochloride; or anyone suffering from epilepsy or other seizure disorders.

ALTERNATIVE METHODS TO STOP SMOKING

Alternative medicine is a hot topic in the country today and there are two forms of alternative or complementary treatment that may interest parents and teens. They are hypnosis and acupuncture. Ask your doctor for a referral to a qualified, experienced hypnotherapist if this approach is of interest to you or your teen. There is evidence that hypnosis can be helpful for many people who want to quit smoking.

Acupuncture, an ancient technique used in traditional Chinese medicine, is also useful for some people who are trying to stop smoking. If this method interests you, ask your doctor or other health practitioner for a recommendation. Many HMOs and other health plans now offer acupuncture as a treatment option. Make sure you see a trained, experienced acupuncturist.

Neither of these alternative approaches offers a cure. And both work best as part of a serious smoking cessation program. The major effort must be made by the smoker who is attempting to quit. No therapy, drug, or treatment will do the job for you.

If a teen is reluctant or unable to participate in a formal smoking cessation program, or is of an independent mind and determined to structure his or her own program, there are many helpful workbooks available through libraries and bookstores to assist and guide them. One excellent example is *The Stop Smoking Workbook—Your Guide to Healthy Quitting* by Anita Maximin, Psy.D., and Lori Stevic-Rust, Ph.D.

This book was written for anybody who is ready to quit smoking. It offers information about smoking and research into smoking, building a foundation for quitting, assessing smoking's impact on health, coping with obstacles to smoking, developing quitting strategies, and dealing with relapse. It is a practical, hands-on workbook that can be a useful tool for any teen who is attempting to quit.

The specific information contained in the workbook is essentially the same as that outlined here and used in a wide variety of smoking cessation programs. However, through quizzes, self-tests, exercises, and question-and-answer sections, the authors take the reader through the process of quitting in an active way. A teen using this book is able to write down her thoughts and reactions, answer and self-score the tests, and gradually compile an ongoing record of her attempt to stop smoking. Workbooks such as this one provide a structure that may be useful for teens who find it difficult to create their own journals about quitting or to keep a record in their diaries. Parents who familiarize themselves with books such as these can alert their teens to their existence and guide them in choosing the one that seems best.

THE REALITY OF RELAPSE

Relapse is a major problem that all smoking cessation programs handle. It is also a phenomenon that most parents will face when their teens try to stop smoking. Keep in mind that complete relapse or experiencing "slips" (i.e., puffing on a friend's cigarette or having a few cigarettes) are often part of the process. If your teen stops and then starts smoking again, it's no reason to panic or despair. The typical smoker needs from four to five attempts at quitting before stopping smoking successfully. A recent Harris poll of 1,002 smokers who were attempting to quit found that most required five attempts before they succeeded. In addition, the poll revealed that most of those surveyed started smoking again within thirty days of stopping.

If your teen relapses completely or has a slip, encourage him to think about starting over again right away. Teens may be embarrassed and need some time to get over the negative feelings associated with having failed in their attempt. That's only natural and, fortunately, teens have time on their side.

Parents can support their children by exploring with them the factors that led them to smoke again. There is much to be gained by looking at the emotions, stresses, and social factors that made your son or daughter reach for a cigarette. By focusing on the triggers that led to lighting up a cigarette, teens can learn to do better the next time. On a future attempt at quitting, red flags will go up when a teen recognizes a situation or feeling that led to relapse in the past. This red flag can alert your son or daughter to take action that will prevent a recurrence of the relapse. The teen may exercise or meditate to relieve stress, or pick up the phone and call a friend or family member for support, instead of seeking solace in a smoke.

Teens who have relapsed don't start over again from ground zero. Every time a teen doesn't light up, she is developing the strength needed to quit for good. When a teen postpones smoking for a few hours, stops smoking for a day or a week, or even quits for a month or more, he or she is taking important steps that will pay off down the road and lead to stopping smoking successfully.

Quitting is not an error-free or mistake-free process. In stopping smoking, as in most of life, we learn some of our most important lessons by looking at the mistakes we make. A hitter in baseball who is struggling at the plate studies videotapes of himself swinging at bad pitches, striking out, or popping the ball up with the winning run in scoring position. The good player doesn't hide from his mistakes. He looks closely at what he is doing at bat to identify what is wrong with his swing so that he can correct it. This is true in baseball, basketball, football, tennis, and every other sport. It is true in science, the arts, education, engineering, architecture, business—in any human endeavor. And it is true when attempting to stop smoking.

Relapse isn't a reason to give up or to throw in the towel. It is cause to dig in and start over again with even more energy, enthusiasm, and determination. Probably the best thing a parent can do for a teen who relapses is to guide him back to the basics of smoking cessation, whether that be through a self-help book, a formal organized program, or an independent strategy the teen devises for himself based on the information about quitting that is widely available today. Quitting doesn't come easy. But anyone *can* quit.

Stopping smoking is one of the most difficult things for anyone to do. Teens need to know this. They also need to know that quitting smoking is one of the single-most important things they can do to create a healthy and happy life for themselves. Big Tobacco tries to brainwash people into fighting for the "freedom *to* smoke," that is, the freedom to be addicted to a lethal but legal product. Parents can support their teens in a much more positive battle, the fight to achieve freedom *from* smoking.

It is often said that it is important in life to learn to choose your battles. Which battle does your teen want to fight and win—the battle for freedom to smoke or the battle for freedom from smoking? Parents who support their teens' struggles to stop smoking help their teens make a vital decision—choosing health over disease. In so doing, parents help their daughters and sons make the most fundamental decision of all—to choose Life over Death.

CHAPTER SIX
Resources

THE INTERNET

When asked why he robbed banks, the notorious bank robber Willie Sutton replied, "Because that's where the money is." Why start a resource section with information about sites on the Internet? Because that's where the teens are.

Teenagers love the Internet and there is a tremendous amount of information, interaction, and support available to them through the many, many Web sites devoted to the entire spectrum of smoking issues. Like the teenagers themselves, the Internet is a growing, evolving, maturing organism. The Web sites listed here may still be around and thriving or long gone when you look for them. Or the Web sites may still exist but be located at a new address. And, undoubtedly, new Web sites that will be of great help to your teen are being developed and going on-line as this book is being written. Don't worry. They know how to surf the net and will find their way to what is cool and helpful.

On the Internet, your teenager can get in touch with other teens all over the world who are also quitting smoking. Your daughter or son can learn about the many excellent organizations and programs that are out there with a lot to offer. And the Internet isn't just for kids. There is a lot going on that can be of great value to parents as well. If you have "computerphobia," or think that the Internet is beyond you, swallow your pride and ask your teen to show you how it works.

If you don't own a computer or are not hooked up to the

Internet, you can probably go on-line at your local library. You don't have to live in a big city or a wealthy suburb to do so either. Small towns and rural areas are often far ahead of their urban and suburban brethren when it comes to the Internet.

There is a wide range of material out there in cyberspace. Not all of it is positive. Some Web sites about smoking actually promote smoking. Don't worry. The novelty of weird and sensational Web sites soon wears thin. And the usefulness of good Web sites, and the excitement of making a connection with other teens, will prove far more alluring. Among the many Web sites available are:

- Campaign for Tobacco-Free Kids: http://www.tobaccofreekids.org
- American Cancer Society: http://www.cancer.org
- American Lung Association: http://www.lungusa.org
- American Heart Association: http://www.amhrt.org/heartg/tobta.html
- KidsHealth (Nemours Foundation): http://www.kidshealth.org
- Action on Smoking and Health: http://www.ash.org
- Washington DOC (Doctors Ought to Care): http://www.kickbutt.org
- Massachusetts Tobacco Education Clearinghouse: http://www.quitnet.org
- The Tobacco BBS: http://www.tobacco.org
- Agency for Health Care Policy and Research Publications Clearinghouse: http://www.ahcpr.gov/
- Dr. Koop: http://www.drkoop.com/tobacco

Smoking Cessation Programs

Here are a few examples of reputable smoking cessation programs:

American Cancer Society
FreshStart Program
1599 Clifton Road NE
Atlanta, GA 30329
1-800-ACS-2345
Fax: 404-248-1780
For information, call the national office or check your local phone directory for the nearest division or unit.

American Council on Science
  and Health
1995 Broadway, 16th floor
New York, NY 10023-5860
212-362-7044

American Dental Association
211 East Chicago Avenue
Chicago, IL 60611
312-440-2500

American Lung Association
Freedom from Smoking Program
1740 Broadway
New York, NY 10019-4374
212-315-8700
America Online Keyword: ALA

American Heart Association
7272 Greenville Avenue
Dallas, TX 75231
800-AHA-USA1

Americans for Non-Smokers
  Rights
2530 San Pablo Avenue, Suite J
Berkeley, CA 97402
510-841-3032
Fax: 510-841-7702
http://www.no-smoke.org

Centers for Disease Control
and Prevention
Office on Smoking and Health
4770 Buford Highway NE
Mail Stop K-50
Atlanta, GA 30341-3724
800-CDC-1311
404-488-5705

Coalition on Smoking and Health
1150 Connecticut Avenue NW
Suite 820
Washington, DC 20036
202-452-1184
Fax: 202-452-1417

Community Intervention Inc.
529 South Seventh Street
Suite 570
Minneapolis, MN 55415
612-332-6537

Doctors Ought to Care (DOC)
561 S. Kirby Drive, Suite 440
Houston, TX 77005
713-798-7729
800-362-9340

Health Promotion Resource
Center
Stanford Center for Research
in Disease Prevention
1000 Welch Road
Palo Alto, CA 94304-1885

National Cancer Institute
800-4CANCER

National Center for
Tobacco-Free Kids
1707 L Street, NW, Suite 800
Washington, DC 20036
202-296-5469
Fax: 202-296-5427

Nicotine Anonymous World
Services
P.O. Box 591777
San Francisco, CA 94159-1777
415-750-0328

Seventh-Day Adventists
Breathe Free Plan
Narcotics Education, Inc.
12501 Old Columbia Pike
Silver Spring, MD 20904-1608
800-548-8700

Stop Teenage Addiction to
Tobacco (STAT)
511 East Columbus Avenue
Springfield, MA 01105
413-732-7828
Fax: 413-732-4219

Selected Reading List

There are many excellent books on smoking and quitting smoking available in the library and in bookstores. A few are mentioned here, along with two publications geared for teens.

Nicoteen: The Don't Smoke Magazine
Scholastic, Inc.
730 Broadway
New York, NY 10003
800-631-1586

Tobacco-Free Youth Reporter
STAT (Stop Teenage Addiction to Smoking)
511 East Columbus Avenue
Springfield, MA 01105
413-732-7828
Fax: 413-732-4219

7 Steps to a Smoke-Free Life by Edwin B. Fisher, Jr., Ph.D., with Toni L. Goldfarb (Wiley, 1997).

The Stop Smoking Workbook—Your Guide to Healthy Quitting by Anita Maximin, Psy.D., and Lori Stevic-Rust, Ph.D., (New Harbinger Publications, Inc., 1996).

The American Cancer Society's "FreshStart": 21 Days to Stop Smoking by Dee Burton, Ph.D. (Pocket Books, 1986).